"Maya Kaimal needs no introduction; she is a household name all over America. You go to a grocery store and are craving Indian food, and her sauces beckon you and make you into an Indian cook, which is exactly what her new must-have book *Indian Flavor Every Day* does. It is an amazing compilation created from a lifetime of celebrating the beauty of one of the most ancient and diverse cuisines in the world."

—**MANEET CHAUHAN,** chef, restaurateur, and author of *Chaat*

"Simple yet not simplistic, Maya Kaimal's latest book is great for anyone looking to add more South Asian flavors into their rotation. Maya concisely coaches you through the cuisine's foundations and then makes them stick with flavorful keepers."

—**ANDREA NGUYEN,** author of *Vietnamese Food Any Day* and *Ever-Green Vietnamese*

"This brilliant and beautiful book breaks down Maya's way of cooking Indian food into easy-to-understand nuggets of information that can be applied to almost every recipe. It sent me immediately into the kitchen because there's a freshness and versatility to Maya's cooking that is right up my alley, and I suspect many others' too."

—**SUSAN SPUNGEN,** author of *Open Kitchen: Inspired Food for Casual Gatherings*

"*Indi... clas... who... confidence. The book is a brilliant collection of irresistible recipes with a wealth of kitchen tips that will elevate your cooking."

—**GRACE YOUNG,** author of *Stir-Frying to the Sky's Edge*

"In *Indian Flavor Every Day*, Maya Kaimal delivers a bounty of personal and engaging recipes, broadens your understanding of spice blends like masala, and creatively combines cuisines that have influenced her throughout her life. I've been cooking from Maya's work for twenty years, and I'm thrilled to have a whole new batch of recipes that will inhabit my kitchen for the next twenty years!"

—**AMANDA HESSER,** founder of *Food52*

"Maya Kaimal's food reminds me of Indian home cooking—comforting and joyful! This is a book richly steeped in flavor and love."

—**NIK SHARMA,** James Beard finalist and author of *The Flavor Equation* and *Season*

"For years, I have relied on Maya for insights into Indian cooking, and *Indian Flavor Every Day* captures so many of the foundational techniques that have made me a better cook. This book clearly distills the vast knowledge of so many Indian cooks into clear, actionable recipes to inspire cooking on any night of the week."

—**CHRIS MOROCCO,** *Bon Appétit* food director

INDIAN FLAVOR
EVERY DAY

INDIAN FLAVOR EVERY DAY

Simple Recipes and Smart Techniques to Inspire

Maya Kaimal

Photographs by Eva Kolenko

Clarkson Potter/Publishers
New York

For my husband, Guy, with all my love.

And for my mother, Lorraine, who always
fed me exceptionally well.

CONTENTS

DALS AND CHICKPEAS

MEAT AND SEAFOOD

RICE, NOODLES, AND BREAD

SWEET BITES

BASICS

INDIAN FLAVOR IN OUR LIVES

Indian food has always fascinated me, from watching my aunty in her South Indian kitchen as a girl to dreaming up new products for the company I founded nearly twenty years ago. Every day I'm either cooking it, eating it, reading or writing about it, or growing a business around it—often all of the above. So when I hear trend forecasters claim year after year that Indian will be the Next Big Cuisine, I just smile. Because even though I suspect it will never have one bust-out moment, Indian food *is* being seen—and not just in a tiny section of the supermarket or on take-out menus. Thanks to the legions of Indian food writers who are lending their perspectives to print and social media, and to the chefs who are getting bolder about sharing their regional and homestyle versions of Indian dishes, this vivid cuisine is now getting the love it deserves, in all its complex glory.

At the same time that Indian food is moving into the mainstream conversation, Americans are cooking and eating in ways that are rapidly changing. The pandemic encouraged us all to cook at home more and stretch our skills, and we are naturally moving toward eating more plants and fewer animals—something Indians have been doing for millennia. In our new normal we need inspiration for dinner more than ever, and that's where Indian food comes to the rescue!

In *Indian Flavor Every Day*, I aim to help you take pleasure in putting Indian flavors on your table in all kinds of ways, just as I've always done with my business, Maya Kaimal Foods, where my goal is to make delicious, quality Indian food both convenient and approachable. While time-saving solutions can be lifesavers, cooking from scratch—with all its aromas, pops, and sizzles—brings its own rewards, turning a daily ritual into an opportunity for discovery and delicious surprises. The recipes here reflect my personal ongoing quest to weave Indian flavors into my family's Western mealtime routine. Why not swirl some popped mustard seeds into a butternut squash soup? How about serving charred carrots with a gingery yogurt sauce next to your roasted chicken, or add a pinch of garam masala to your cookie dough?

Indian food has a reputation for being intimidating. The key to doing all of this with confidence lies in understanding a few simple techniques that I lay out for you in these pages. Before you know it, you'll be mixing up masalas (spice blends) and sautéing them with care to soften their raw edges. I'll show you how toasting shredded coconut adds a new dimension to your cooking. I'll give you foolproof tips for cooking flavorful dals. And you'll love making one of the foundations of Indian flavor—tarka, where you sizzle whole spices in oil, opening up an entire universe of possibility for seasoning food with ease. Some recipes employ the tarka technique as a first step to give your cooking oil a lively boost, while others use it at the end as an exhilarating garnish. It's a wonderful method, and I hope you'll want to start using it all the time, like I do! As you purchase a few ingredients for your pantry and embrace the techniques in this book, I promise you will soon have a comfort level with Indian food you didn't believe was possible.

Indian recipes are also known for requiring many ingredients and steps. To address the often intimidatingly long ingredient list, I did a few things: I limited the use of ingredients that aren't essential to a good outcome, and I broke the ingredient list into segments with headings, like "Tarka" or "Sauce," to show you at a glance how to build the dish. Furthermore, these headings clearly correspond to the steps in the method. I also identify the main "masala" for each dish that has a spice blend, because spices are the heart and soul of Indian food, and when you know how to use them, you understand why Indian food is a symphonic weave of notes and layers, creating its own unique taste. By highlighting the blends you will quickly know the dish's flavor profile: will it be simple or complex, hot or gentle? Once you understand the role of the masala, and how the ingredient groupings work together to build flavor, the ingredient list will seem less daunting.

Unlike when I was growing up, most of the key ingredients in Indian cuisine, like coconut milk, coconut oil, ghee, basmati rice, cilantro, and fresh chilies, are now supermarket staples. There are a few specialized items you will not find at the grocery store, but I have kept them to a minimum. Fortunately, items such as fresh curry leaves, brown or black mustard seeds, tamarind, and chickpea flour are often carried by health food stores, while other things like chaat masala and urad dal will need to be purchased at an Indian market or online. See the Sources section on page 31 for a guide to what you can get where. And with the exception of fresh curry leaves and fresh green chilies, all the ingredients have long shelf lives, so once you have them in your pantry, you can easily pull together the dishes in this book.

The recipes in *Indian Flavor Every Day* are a mix of traditional dishes and twists on those traditions, because that's my favorite way to cook. Some traditional recipes, like lamb kofta, pakoras, dal tarka, saag paneer, chicken Chettinad, and pork vindaloo, have withstood the test of time for good reason. And though they have been streamlined to remove the harder-to-obtain ingredients, the essence of these long-established favorites remains true, and when you make them, you will know immediately why they are so well loved.

The "twist" category of recipes begins with classic ideas that get used in my kitchen in new ways, like brushing a tandoori marinade on cauliflower steaks, or drizzling tamarind chutney on asparagus, or making a veggie burger out of bonda, a favorite Indian street snack. Since forever, cooks have been applying well-honed techniques to new ingredients, so now I'm sharing my favorites with you. And since it feels like we're all on a never-ending quest to make our vegetables interesting, many of the recipes here give you new ways to think about your produce, from cauliflower to green beans, Brussels sprouts, broccoli, or whatever looks good at your local farmers' market. Each becomes something special when you apply the Indian touch.

everyone's dietary needs and also deliver a flavor payoff. This book is the secret trick you've been looking for, because most of the recipes are dairy-free or can easily be converted with a little tweak, and plant-based protein is the name of the game in the "Dals and Chickpeas" chapter (page 131). Wheat does not figure prominently in the book, and if avoiding carbs is your thing, I promise you'll find happiness among the myriad vegetable and meat dishes. All of these attributes are *exactly* what make Indian cuisine so very relevant at this moment: it offers so many richly flavored and textured options that can keep everyone happy and well fed.

Something else that happens at my house is that we eat a lot of scrumptious food from the tropical Indian state of Kerala, where my father grew up. My affection for the region runs deep, and it seasons every chapter of this book with coconut milk, curry leaves, tart tamarind, toasty mustard seeds, and a delicate, aromatic version of garam masala that scents dishes from savory to sweet—all signature flavors of this lush area of southern India. My Aunty Kamala took an interest in teaching me how to get the utmost flavor from these very special ingredients so that I could re-create her fish curries and thorens (vegetable sautés) back in the United States. Kerala is also uniquely famous for its meat dishes, and when you taste Peppery Beef Curry (page 166) or Rich Kerala Egg Roast (page 161), you'll be surprised and delighted. There's a tropical lushness to this food I can't resist, and I will always be inspired by these alluring aromas and flavors. I hope you love them, too!

I am especially excited to share the dessert recipes here. They don't resemble traditional Indian sweets, but instead are familiar American dessert forms with a hint of India. For example, I put garam masala in the pastry crust of a chocolate tart, brush ghee and chai spices on grilled pineapple, and enhance pots de crème with South Indian coffee. And the cookie recipes offer subtle and satisfying spice flavors to complement any Indian-accented meal.

In my home, planning dinner means accommodating vegetarian, vegan, lactose-free, gluten-free, low-cholesterol, and omnivore appetites, and there are only four of us! I know there are countless other families like ours, looking for foods that fit

Finally, while the recipes in *Indian Flavor Every Day* have been carefully thought through and tested to be delicious as presented, I hope they will serve as inspirations for you. My wish is that once you have the ingredients and get a feel for the tarka technique and mixing masalas, you can embark on your own adventures, applying an Indian touch to any of your favorite ingredients or meals.

For as long as I can remember, Indian flavors have had an outsized role in my imagination. I was raised in a multicultural home in Boston and later Boulder, Colorado, with a mother from New England and a father from South India. My parents raised me; my sister, Padma; and my brother, Narayan, to prize eating together at the dining room table every night. Most days we ate my mother Lorraine's excellent cooking, as she did deep dives into the cookbooks of Julia Child and Joyce Chen. Meanwhile my father, Chandran, a physicist, used his scientific method to experiment in the kitchen on weekends, expertly re-creating the dishes of his native Kerala, despite having to rely on dried bay leaves for curry leaves and lemon juice in place of tamarind. He would test his recipes on us, and when they met his high standards, they were neatly typed up and put into a three-ring binder. That binder of recipes followed me around and helped set me on my path in the food world: I cooked out of it in my college dorm, I used it to start an Indian catering side hustle when I moved to New York City, and the recipes helped me land my first cookbook contract for *Curried Favors*.

By the time I wrote my second book, *Savoring the Spice Coast of India*, I was traveling to India on my own, learning ever more from Aunty Kamala, my cousin Padma, family friends, and kind chefs who invited me into their kitchens. I was also working in publishing as a photo editor, ultimately landing my dream job at *Saveur* magazine. Around that time, I met my husband, the writer Guy Lawson, who, thanks to his upbringing in Toronto and Australia and years spent studying in England, was a firm fan of Indian food. Soon after we married, we launched an Indian sauce business based on my recipes from our apartment in Brooklyn. To spice things up further, I gave birth to twins the same year! We didn't know much about running a business, but I devoted all my efforts to using the techniques shared here to create time-saving products that delivered maximum Indian flavor. Sales picked up, and we likewise picked up and moved from Brooklyn to New York's Hudson Valley, the very spot where our sauces were being produced by a small upstate manufacturer.

We still live in a small town on the Hudson River, two working parents of busy teenagers, short on time, and trying to pull dinner together every day. We eat all kinds of different dishes in our home, but when I find myself yearning for something truly comforting, homemade, and time-saving, I reach for the jar of mustard seeds, a splash of coconut milk, or a fresh green chili to liven up a dish. In *Indian Flavor Every Day*, I hope to give you the confidence and the tools to explore my favorite cuisine's ingredients, so you can create your own solutions for your dinnertime and take pleasure in discovering the transformative power of these wonderful flavors.

Clockwise from top left: My grandmother Ambuja; my mother in Belmont, Massachusetts; our family in Kerala, India; visiting I'timad-ud-Daulah's Tomb, Agra, India; with my parents in New York; with my Aunty Kamala in Kerala; cooking with my father; having a special meal at Aunty Kamala (back left) and Uncle Chinnappan's home, Kottayam, Kerala.

STOCKING YOUR INDIAN FLAVOR PANTRY

This section walks you through what you'll need to easily create Indian flavors and is divided into these categories: Fresh Produce, Spices, and Pantry Staples. And since I want you to make this food easily and often, most of these ingredients can be purchased at a supermarket or health food store. The few items that require special sourcing are included in the resources on page 31, and some very decent substitutes to use in a pinch are listed on page 30. I also suggest the tools that will be useful to have on hand. Once your kitchen is kitted out, you'll have the elements you need to make this food for a good long time!

Fresh Produce

Here are a few fresh ingredients that will really make your food sparkle. So much flavor is derived from fresh chilies, curry leaves, cilantro, garlic, and ginger in my recipes that it's good to understand the ins and outs of each and how to maximize their life in your refrigerator or freezer.

FRESH CILANTRO

Thankfully cilantro is widely available, unlike when I was growing up and a special trip to Boston's Chinatown was required! It's worth noting that Indians always use the *stems* as well as the leaves, so you'll see my recipes call for chopped leaves and tender stems. The stems contribute a refreshing flavor and crisp texture, and you will love cooking with them—if you don't already.

STORAGE

Refrigerate
My tried-and-true approach for getting 7 to 10 days out of fresh cilantro is to wash it as soon as I get it home, put it in a salad spinner or bowl filled with ice water, and let it sit for about 10 minutes to hydrate. Spin it dry, then lay it out on a dish towel to air-dry. When dry but still fluffy, place it in a plastic or glass container lined on all six sides with paper towels, seal tightly, and refrigerate. You can give it a refresh by washing it again after a few days.

FRESH CURRY LEAVES

This aromatic herb, also called kari patta, is a signature flavor in South Indian cooking, much the way basil is to Italian food. Not to be confused with curry powder (a colonial misnaming coincidence), it has a sturdy texture and responds well to being sizzled in oil as part of a tarka. It has a bitter grapefruit–bell peppery aroma like nothing else. It is sold in refrigerated packets in Indian grocery stores, Asian markets, and some health food stores. The sprigs contain ten to twenty leaves, which can vary from ½ to 1½ inches long. These recipes assume the larger leaf, so if yours are small, double the amount called for.

STORAGE

Refrigerate
This is by far the best way to keep curry leaves, since they lose their potency in the freezer and have zero flavor when dried. Two tips: First, I choose not to wash curry leaves because it causes them to deteriorate faster. Second, keep them on the stem; they stay hydrated when attached. Inspect your sprigs, discard any bruised leaves, and blot away all moisture. Wrap them in fresh paper towels (the leaves can be stacked) and place them in a reusable zippered bag, pressing out all the air. They should last a month.

Freeze

Frozen curry leaves are better than no curry leaves, so keep some in the freezer for when you're in a pinch. Again, do not wash the leaves before freezing because it turns them brown. Do strip them off the stem, removing any dark ones. Blot them dry and place them in a flat reusable zippered bag with all the air pressed out to prevent freezer burn. You'll get 6 months of semi-decent flavor from them.

GARLIC AND GINGER

These are cornerstone flavors in Indian cooking, so often used together that you can buy garlic-ginger paste at Indian stores, which is a time-saver, but it does contain preservatives. I prefer the taste of fresh, or in a pinch I use my homemade frozen stash (see below). And I keep both ginger and garlic unwrapped in my refrigerator's vegetable drawer.

STORAGE

Freeze

The following method will help you save time on prep, with minimal loss of flavor if used within a few months. Finely mince approximately ½ cup of each (a head of garlic, a small hand of ginger) separately in a food processor. Store in separate glass or plastic jars in the freezer. I recommend taking them out of the freezer 5 to 10 minutes before using so they are easier to scoop out.

FRESH GREEN CHILIES

It's hard to believe chili peppers, or capsicums, have been part of Indian cooking only since the Portuguese introduced them in the sixteenth century. But their decisive heat is essential to the flavor balance of Indian cooking. And while there are countless varieties used across the subcontinent, I'm focusing on small, hot green chilies here, with three suggestions—serranos being my strong favorite. The heat of a chili is measured in Scoville units, named for Wilbur Scoville, an American pharmacist who devised a scale for measuring the water units required to neutralize one unit of ground-up chili. The Scoville ratings are provided for the chilies below to show their relative potency, with the higher numbers representing hotter peppers.

SERRANO

This is the variety of fresh green chili that most closely matches the size and taste of what my family in India uses, so it is my first choice. It is the size of a pinkie finger and has semi-thick skin and a good amount of seeds. And it has impressive but balanced firepower that makes your whole mouth glow—in a good way (we love those endorphins!). If you can't find them, substitute jalapeños or Thai bird chilies (see page 18 for equivalencies). Between 1 and 2 teaspoons of chopped serrano (with seeds) will get your attention! If you like a milder curry, remove the seeds and white pith. If you omit it altogether, you will miss out on the warm note that is an important part of Indian flavor.

))) 10,000–25,000 SCOVILLE UNITS

JALAPEÑO

This is the mildest of the fresh chilies I'm recommending, and it has the advantage of being widely available. Jalapeños can range from 2 to 4 inches and have thick, glossy, dark green skins and the faint taste of green bell pepper. The seeds are generally low impact but can occasionally be feisty. Buy the littlest ones you can (the smaller, the hotter) and use one and a half to two times the amount of a serrano.

)) 3,000–10,000 SCOVILLE UNITS

THAI BIRD

This 1½-inch-long chili gives an instantaneous sharp heat that quickly fills your whole mouth and lingers. They have thin skins and loads of fiery seeds and pith that never disappoint, so use three-quarters to half the amount of a serrano.

))))) 100,000–250,000 SCOVILLE UNITS

STORAGE

Refrigerate
Keep chilies fresh for up to 1 month by following these steps: Rinse well and spread them out on a dish towel. When completely dry, pull off their stems and calyxes (the base of the stem), because this is the first place mold will grow. Wrap them up in paper towels, leaving no gaps, and place them snugly in an airtight plastic container or reusable zippered bag with all the air pressed out. Rewrap them each time you take one out, and if the paper towel feels moist, replace it with a fresh, dry one.

Freeze
If you have more chilies than you can use up in a month, store them in the freezer in a reusable zippered bag (no paper towel required) for up to 6 months. This is not my favorite method, because they lose some of their heat and also break apart when cooked. But it's nice to have a stash in the freezer for emergencies!

HOW TO SPLIT A WHOLE GREEN CHILI

Many recipes instruct you to "split" a whole green chili before adding it to the recipe—a trick that's common in Indian cooking. This doesn't mean to literally split it into two halves, but rather partially bisect it starting from the bottom tip and stopping short of the top by about half an inch or enough to keep it intact. This allows the chili to release some, but not all, of its heat and seeds into the dish, providing a more gentle effect than when minced. It also gives you the flexibility to remove the chili partway through cooking if you feel the dish is hot enough.

Since fresh chilies vary in heat level, it's nice to know if you have a tame one or a scorcher before you start cooking.

Here's an easy trick for learning that without lighting your tongue on fire! Cut off the top end of the chili to expose the seed area, swipe the tip of your pinkie finger (or a digit you won't accidentally rub in your eye) across the cut end, then gently touch it to the tip of your tongue.

You'll have your answer in a nanosecond and here's why: the source of the chili's heat is a compound called capsaicin, which is concentrated in the capsaicin glands, or the pale, pithy part the seeds cling to, and cutting off the top exposes this area. (Many people think the seeds are the hottest part, but it turns out the pith is hotter.)

If you feel an instantaneous but short-lived burning on your tongue, you know you have a live one, and you should follow the recipe as written. If it takes a beat or two until you detect the heat, you have a moderately hot chili, so you may want to increase the quantity. If you feel nothing at all, repeat the experiment to confirm that the chili is low in firepower, and move on until you find a hot one.

QUICK TIPS
- Capsaicin is oil based, so water won't cool the flame.
- Drink milk or eat yogurt or starchy foods to cool off your tingly mouth.
- Thoroughly wash your hands with soap after handling chilies.
- Wear gloves if you're supersensitive.
- If you prefer mild heat, use the apex (tip) of the chili.
- Generally speaking, the smaller the chili, the greater the heat.

Spices

Spices are undeniably essential to Indian cooking, and if you take good care of them by keeping them in airtight containers away from the light, they will maintain flavor for a long time. How long? That question is hotly (pun intended) debated, but in my experience the answer is around two years for ground spices, and up to five years for whole ones. Some experts feel that's too long, and if you have the wherewithal to clean out your spice cupboard on an annual basis, go for it! You'll note I suggest pre-ground spices in many cases because of their convenience. But please grind your own from whole if you prefer. Your curry will be just a little bit more robust—in a good way. For the meat and seafood curries, I choose to use the ground form of cinnamon, whole cloves, or cardamom pods because I personally don't like biting into them. Whole seeds such as mustard, cumin, and fennel, on the other hand, are used throughout this book, particularly in the tarkas. Below is a list of all the spices you should have on hand to make these recipes.

ASAFETIDA

This tan powdered rhizome has a strong sulfur-onion aroma when raw. Used sparingly but effectively (⅛ to ¼ teaspoon is enough for most recipes), its taste mellows after it has been sizzled in oil. Asafetida is believed to make beans more digestible, so it is often used in dals. Find it at Indian stores, sometimes labeled as hing.

BLACK PEPPERCORNS

Look for Kerala-grown varieties, sold under names like Tellicherry, Malabar, or Aranya. Kerala has the best growing conditions, yielding big peppercorns with a sharp sunbaked bite. Regardless of the variety, its pleasantly bitter heat is best appreciated when freshly ground.

BROWN OR BLACK MUSTARD SEEDS

There's no significant difference between the brown and black seeds (*left*)—I always look for whichever is larger because those will give more flavor when dropped in hot oil as part of a tarka (the tan ones are less pungent). The seeds' moisture causes them to explode when heated, releasing a nutty popcorn-like aroma.

CARDAMOM, PODS AND GROUND

Look for green pods, which are more aromatic than the bleached white ones and less smoky and intense than black cardamom. The powerful woody-sweet-menthol fragrance is an important ingredient in garam masala and Indian desserts. Pre-ground is convenient if you need a large quantity. If grinding your own, crush the pods with a rolling pin, discard the outer husks, and grind only the tiny seeds inside. It is acceptable to grind the husks and the seeds, but the flavor will be less intense.

CAYENNE

Made from dry-roasted cayenne peppers, this brick-red powder (*left*) is widely available. It has a harsh, sharp edge that mellows a little when cooked, but Indians say if you use too much it will "catch in the throat." Using ¼ to ½ teaspoon for four people will deliver decent heat.

))) 38,000–50,000 SCOVILLE UNITS

CHAAT MASALA

This tart, tangy spice blend is used on raw salads and chaat snacks and can be purchased from Indian sources. Its unique flavor comes from a funky blend that includes black salt, sour mango, cumin, and black pepper.

CINNAMON, GROUND

Look for Sri Lankan (Ceylonese) or Vietnamese cinnamon for their exceptional flavor. In Indian cooking, cinnamon is frequently part of a trio with clove and cardamom, since their flavors are so harmonious. The combination is used in garam masala, as well as in vegetable and meat curries and dals.

CLOVE, GROUND

Clove, with its woody-hot-sweet personality, can overwhelm a dish, so it's best used sparingly. Even in small amounts, it is a crucial part of the Indian spice matrix (see Cinnamon, ground).

CORIANDER, GROUND

The earthy-citrusy taste of ground coriander manages to both lift a curry and give it gravity. It's especially well suited to meat dishes, providing both flavor and thickness to the sauce. This is used often and in larger quantities than most spices, so the ease of pre-ground is very convenient.

CUMIN, WHOLE SEEDS AND GROUND

Warm, toasty, and a little bitter, cumin is a foundational flavor in Indian cuisine. Whole seeds are used in tarkas for dals and vegetables and in the blend panch phoron; ground is used in every category of cooking, save desserts. Its character can change significantly depending on whether it is whole, toasted, ground, or fried, and all these forms are used in my recipes. And like coriander, you'll use it often and will appreciate having jars of both ground and whole seeds on hand.

FENNEL SEEDS

These plump pale green seeds (*left*) have a hard shell that, when crushed, releases a sweet licorice scent. Indians chew them as a breath freshener. I always prefer freshly grinding them for optimal flavor. Fennel is an important back note, especially in meat and fish dishes, though a little goes a long way.

FENUGREEK SEEDS

Square, golden fenugreek seeds (actually beans) add a distinct bitter butterscotch note that can be picked up in the aroma of generic curry powders. It's one of the five seeds in the blend panch phoron, and it's important in South Indian dishes like rasam and fish curries. Use sparingly and purchase from Indian stores.

KASHMIRI CHILI POWDER

This spice is named for the northern state where it is ostensibly grown (but it can be from other regions as well) and celebrated for its gorgeous red color and moderate firepower. The taste is similar to paprika but with more kick. It's available through Indian specialty spice sources. Up to ¾ teaspoon will not overwhelm your dish. See Chili Powder Confusion, opposite, for an easy swap.

🌶 1,500–2,000 SCOVILLE UNITS

NIGELLA SEEDS

Also called kalonji, these tiny black seeds punch above their weight, bringing a pleasant bitter-onion taste to vegetables and flatbreads. They are one of the five spices in panch phoron. And while they resemble black sesame seeds, they have a more assertive flavor. They are available from Indian and specialty spice sources.

DON'T HAVE KASHMIRI CHILI POWDER?

No worries! This blend is a good equivalent to give you bright paprika color with smoldering cayenne heat. Mix up a little bottle and keep it handy: 3 tablespoons sweet paprika and 1 tablespoon cayenne.

PAPRIKA, SWEET

This variety of paprika is made from fully ripened mild red peppers. The seeds are removed before the pods are ground, ensuring a mellow heat. It's not recommended to use it interchangeably with hot or smoked paprika, as it tastes very different.

250–1,000 SCOVILLE UNITS

RED CHILIES, WHOLE DRIED

There are many varieties of chilies that work well in Indian food, including sannam, desi lal mirch, and chile de arbol, and they can range in color from crimson to deep maroon. They should be about the length of a pinkie finger, and when dropped in hot oil, their skin blisters and browns, producing a smoky, subtle heat. No risk of overdosing here. If you can't find them, use ⅛ teaspoon dried red chili flakes as a substitute for 1 dried chili.

5,000–15,000 SCOVILLE UNITS

RED CHILI FLAKES

Also sold as dried red pepper flakes or crushed red pepper, this form of red chili is easier to find than whole dried pods, so I recommend it as a substitute. But since this form contains more seeds by weight than a whole chili, you only need ⅛ to ¼ teaspoon to give a good spark to a dish.

15,000–30,000 SCOVILLE UNITS

STAR ANISE, WHOLE

These beautiful dried star-shaped pods have a sweet-woody-licorice flavor and should be used with a light hand. Their flavor is important in Kerala Garam Masala (page 224).

TURMERIC, GROUND

Essential to Indian cooking, this golden root has achieved rock-star status because of its many health-promoting properties. But in Indian cooking, it occupies an important yet supporting role, adding bright color but bitter flavor. Too much of a good thing is not always better, so avoid the urge to pile on more turmeric than is called for.

CHILI POWDER CONFUSION

It's common see "chili powder" or "chilli powder" called for in Indian recipes, which is not to be confused with our grocery store "chili powder" that is used for chili con carne (actually a blend including paprika, cumin, and oregano). Indian chili powder is a bright red powder made of mixed chilies and is much milder than cayenne. It is marketed under the name deggi mirch, but unfortunately sources can't agree if it can be used interchangeably with Kashmiri chili or if it is milder than Kashmiri. For this book, if you like to cook with Indian chili powder, I recommend you substitute three times as much as the amount of cayenne, or one and a half times the amount of Kashmiri chili called for in these recipes.

Madras Curry
Powder (page 225)

North Indian Garam
Masala (page 222)

Kerala Garam
Masala
(page 224)

Panch Phoron
(page 226)

Pantry Staples

This section covers the basic building blocks you'll need to have in your cupboard. I'm pleased to report that many items can be easily found at supermarkets and health food stores, or at Indian markets, or online, if needed.

COCONUT
COCONUT OIL, UNREFINED

Also labeled virgin or extra-virgin coconut oil, this gives you the richest coconut flavor, whereas coconut oil loses its aroma when it's refined. It is best kept in the refrigerator, where it will solidify. Soften it in hot water or for a 30-second stint in the microwave.

DRIED UNSWEETENED SHREDDED COCONUT

I recommend buying this with a medium texture, which has a similar consistency to panko bread crumbs. Do not use the types that are coarse and stringy or finely powdered. And *never* use the sweetened variety. Health food stores and Indian sources reliably carry it, and many supermarkets now stock it in their natural food section.

FROZEN UNSWEETENED SHREDDED COCONUT

Frozen shredded coconut has a similar flavor and texture to fresh and can be found in one-pound bags at Indian grocery stores. Since it freezes into a single mass, thaw it in the refrigerator for a few hours prior to breaking off the portion you need (it is safe to refreeze the unused portion). The recipes in this book were designed for dried coconut, so note that frozen doesn't toast as quickly because of its moisture content.

FULL-FAT CANNED COCONUT MILK

Canned coconut milk is a marvelous convenience; the only downsides are that it keeps for only a few days in the refrigerator once opened, and brands with clean labels (i.e., no emulsifiers) tend to separate into watery liquid and solid fat. Regarding the spoiling issue, many of my recipes use less than a can, which is in line with the volume used in my family's food, but I offer solutions when it comes to storing the unused portion. As for the separation, that can be solved by shaking or stirring. My recipes all use full-fat coconut milk, and I recommend buying all-natural brands. So-called lite versions will obviously taste thinner and appear less creamy. Coconut cream can be diluted with 30 percent water to mimic coconut milk. Definitely avoid cream of coconut, which contains sugar and additives and is intended for cocktails.

TIPS FOR FREEZING COCONUT MILK

Save excess coconut milk by freezing it. Pour your extra coconut milk into a glass or plastic container with a tight-fitting lid (leaving a little headspace) and freeze. Defrost it in the refrigerator overnight, or for a quick defrost, place it in a bowl of extremely hot water (don't submerge the container or it might leak) or in the microwave in 30-second increments, shaking it gently between each period. When you defrost it, you may notice separation from the fat clumping together, but don't worry, it isn't "curdled" like milk, and the taste is fine. This will disappear once you add it to your pot and stir it. (Or you can emulsify it in a blender or with a whisk, if you wish.) Avoid vigorously boiling coconut milk, which also causes the fat molecules to bond and appear curdled.

DAL AND CHICKPEAS

The term *dal* (meaning "to split") is used to refer to split pulses in their dried form as well as the stew-like dish made from them.

BLACK LENTILS

These small black beans are also known as beluga lentils because of their resemblance to black caviar. They are very flavorful and thick-skinned, and they turn a deep chocolate brown when cooked and pureed. Health food stores usually stock them.

BLACK URAD (WHOLE)

Urad beans are sold in very different forms, so be sure you are purchasing the whole beans with black skins wherever this version is called for. When fully cooked, their skins will split open to reveal their ivory interiors. Buy these from Indian stores or online, and use them in dal recipes.

CHANA DAL (SPLIT)

Also known as Bengal gram, this is the most common dal in India and is derived from chickpeas that are smaller than the classic tan variety (kabuli chana). When split, they closely resemble yellow split peas but are thicker and rounder. They can be used interchangeably with their split pea cousin, but chana dal has a richer flavor and takes longer to cook.

CHICKPEAS (GARBANZOS), CANNED

Known as kabuli chana (literally, the "chickpea from Kabul") or simply chana, this tan bean with a creamy texture is very versatile and used often in North Indian cooking. The canned form is incredibly convenient, since they otherwise require a long soak and cook time.

RED LENTILS (WHOLE OR SPLIT)

Sold as masoor dal, these salmon-colored lentils are thin and cook quickly. If purchasing them from an Indian store, make sure they are hulled, and feel free to use split or whole in these recipes since there's barely a difference in the cooking time. The color fades from pale orange to tannish yellow when cooked.

TOOR DAL (PIGEON PEAS, SPLIT)

A golden split legume that looks like a thinner version of yellow split peas, this is a very popular dal, especially in South India, and has a pleasant earthy flavor. Indian stores sell an oiled version of this dal, meant to extend its shelf life. Look for the unoiled version, which doesn't require soaking to remove the oil.

WHITE URAD DAL (SPLIT, HULLED)

This is the dal (*left*) most often used as part of a tarka, adding a nutty flavor and crunchy texture once fried in hot oil. Urad dal's black skin has been removed, leaving a small white oval bean. This is also the bean used to make South Indian dosa and idli.

YELLOW MOONG DAL (SPLIT MUNG BEANS, HULLED)
Mung beans come in different colors and forms, but for these recipes you want the split, yellow version with the olive-green skin removed. These easily digestible beans are a favorite in South India, where they are often toasted before being cooked.

YELLOW SPLIT PEAS
Widely available in US markets, these are the dried form of a yellow variety of pea. They are an easily available substitute for either toor dal or chana dal.

FLOUR
CHICKPEA FLOUR

Also labeled garbanzo flour, this is made from tan chickpeas (kabuli chana) and is different from the Indian version called besan, which is made from a type of chickpea known as chana dal (Bengal gram). It's used for fried noodles, to thicken curries, and in desserts; it also makes an excellent rich batter for fried snacks. Chickpea/garbanzo flour is available at natural food stores and some supermarkets, while besan is sold at Indian stores. Both work well, though chickpea flour is coarser and therefore requires more water than besan in batters.

ATTA FLOUR
This golden-beige flour is made from finely milled durum wheat. It's low in gluten and is ideal for making soft South Asian flatbreads like chapatis, parathas, and puris. Find it at Indian stores.

NEUTRAL OIL: CORN, SAFFLOWER, SUNFLOWER, CANOLA
The flavor of the spices and aromatics is paramount, so neutral-tasting oils are a better fit in Indian cooking than, for example, extra-virgin olive oil. Another consideration when choosing a general cooking oil for Indian food is its smoke point, or the temperature at which the oil starts to smoke. Corn, safflower, and sunflower are my top choices for these recipes, except when ghee or coconut oil is called for. Canola is also acceptable but can smell somewhat fishy when heated.

RICE
BASMATI RICE
Celebrated for its baked-earth perfume and extra-long grains, this rice has become an American supermarket staple. Its provenance is the Himalayan foothills, and even though it's now grown domestically, it's hard to compete

with the taste and texture of true basmati from India or Pakistan. Rinsing off the starch in a bowl of water is recommended for a fluffier finished product.

JASMINE RICE

This aromatic long-grain rice with a floral, nutty scent is widely available. The grains are juicy and cook quickly, and while it's grown in Thailand, it's popular all over South Asia. It's flavorful on its own, but I like to use it for highly seasoned rice dishes because its plump grains soak up the flavors more than basmati.

SALT

FINE SEA SALT

Almost all my recipes call for this type, and I use La Baleine fine sea salt from France because it's widely distributed in the United States, has a nice flavor, and melts quickly into the food. You can substitute any brand of granulated sea salt or table salt (but not low-sodium varieties) whenever fine sea salt is listed. If you have Diamond Crystal kosher salt, double the amount; for Morton kosher salt, use 25 percent more.

KOSHER SALT

In some recipes I specifically call for kosher salt, mostly in boiling water or for sprinkling over meat. It's fine to use either Diamond Crystal or Morton since the quantities are not critical. But if you wish to use table salt in place of kosher, use about 25 percent less.

TAMARIND PASTE OR CONCENTRATE

Made from a puckery-tart South Asian fruit with a date-like texture, tamarind is used in many South Indian dishes (especially seafood) much like lemon. But when it comes to purchasing it, the naming conventions are not standardized. Syrups and blocks both use the word *paste*, while liquids can be labeled "paste," "concentrate," or "puree." I advise you to look for tamarind sold in jars that appears like a denser, darker version of molasses. Be sure the label reads 100 percent tamarind; it should be pure fruit processed from a fibrous mass into a smooth puree. Pressed blocks are also acceptable, albeit more cumbersome to work with because they need to be soaked in hot water, mashed, then strained. Whether it's a concentrate or a block, you can use the measurements in this book. If your tamarind contains water and is light brown, however, you should use four times what the recipe calls for. Indian and health food stores stock it.

Ingredient Alternatives

Don't despair if you can't get some of the ingredients. Here are suggested substitutes for the harder-to-find items. The final flavor of your dish will be a little different but still satisfying and worth the effort. All quantities are used 1:1 unless otherwise noted.

Asafetida	Mix equal parts onion powder and garlic powder
Atta flour	Mix 2 parts all-purpose flour and 1 part whole-wheat flour
Black urad dal, whole	Black lentils (beluga lentils)
Brown or black mustard seeds	Yellow mustard seeds
Chaat masala	Mix equal parts toasted ground cumin and fine sea salt
Chana dal	Yellow split peas
Curry leaves, fresh	Use 1 bay leaf when 12 to 15 curry leaves are called for
Fenugreek seeds	Use the equivalent measure of any commercial curry powder containing fenugreek
Kashmiri chili powder	Mix 3 parts sweet paprika and 1 part cayenne
Nigella seeds	Black sesame seeds
Panch phoron	Equal parts mustard seeds, cumin seeds, and black sesame seeds
Split white urad dal	Red lentils (masoor dal)
Tamarind paste or concentrate	Equal parts fresh lemon juice and packed dark brown sugar
Toor dal	Yellow split peas

Sources

As much as I wish every ingredient were available at your local grocery store, it's not the case—yet! But to make the best-tasting versions of these recipes, you will need to get a handful of ingredients from an Indian market or one of these online sources.

ONE-STOP SHOPPING

To set yourself up with everything covered in this chapter, from fresh curry leaves to spices to pantry items (including organic options), use these suppliers for your grocery haul. Specialized Indian vessels like tarka pans and kadais are available through many of these sources as well.

Amazon (www.amazon.com)
Desi Basket (www.desibasket.com; store in Edison, New Jersey)
Kalustyan's (www.foodsofnations.com; store in New York City)
Patel Brothers (www.patelbros.com; store locations nationwide)

FRESH CURRY LEAVES

This fragrant herb is worth seeking out to get the fullest flavor from these recipes. Indian grocery stores usually carry them, but if you don't see them, ask, because they might be in the back. Some health food stores now carry the fresh sprigs in their herb section. Or you can try growing your own plant, but they can be finicky and difficult to grow in North America. Luckily there's always overnight shipping, which works well because (a) they weigh almost nothing and (b) they are sturdy enough to survive out of refrigeration during shipping. Here are some sources that will ship them to you:

Kalustyan's (www.foodsofnations.com)
Rani Brand (www.ranibrand.com)
Umami Cart (www.umamicart.com)

SINGLE SPICES AND SPICE BLENDS

There are so many great options for purchasing small-batch, high-quality spices today that it's hard to narrow down the list. But I've chosen a few good sources to satisfy your spice needs. Note that many of the spice blends in this book, including garam masala, Madras curry powder, and panch phoron, can either be made from scratch or purchased. While I can vouch for the quality of these sources, every vendor has their own formulation, so try to find one that lists their ingredients in an order that most closely matches my recipes for the intended outcome.

Burlap & Barrel (www.burlapandbarrel.com)
Diaspora Co. (www.diasporaco.com)
Kalustyan's (www.foodsofnations.com)
The Spice House (www.thespicehouse.com)

Useful Tools

Small 8-inch frying pan for tarkas and toasting, or a tarka pan

Deep 11- to 12-inch skillet with a lid, or a Dutch oven

Flat-bottomed 12-inch wok with a lid, or a 10-inch kadai (Indian-style wok)

Saucepans: at least one 3- or 4-quart pot, for dals and rice

6- to 8-quart stockpot, for soups and noodles

Food processor or blender; a mini food processor is also useful

Electric spice grinder (i.e., a coffee grinder dedicated to spices; Krups makes a great one) is highly recommended

Mortar and pestle, useful for crushing spices

10 to 12 small prep cups for your mise en place

Measuring spoons: a good set that goes down to ⅛ teaspoon (I suggest having two sets, one for wet and the other for dry ingredients)

Measuring cups: from ¼ cup to 4 cups

Chef's knife

Vegetable peeler

Citrus squeezer

Microplane

Parchment paper

Garam masala (meaning "warm spices") contains ingredients that help provide a feeling of warmth in the sometimes chilly North Indian climate. Most commercial blends labeled "garam masala" contain cinnamon, clove, cardamom, and black pepper, plus less expensive cumin and coriander. My North Indian Garam Masala (page 222) omits the cumin and coriander, so it has a more intense cinnamon-clove-cardamom hit than the store-bought type. Meanwhile, my Kerala Garam Masala (page 224) is distinct from the North Indian version, with fennel and star anise adding a sweet licorice note to the cinnamon, clove, and cardamom combination. Fennel also provides a cooling quality, which is more suited to the lower latitudes. Note that the two masalas are *not* interchangeable, and since the Kerala version is not sold commercially, you'll need to make your own.

FLAVOR-BUILDING TECHNIQUES

Now that you know what to put in your pantry, these pages explain how to get the most out of those ingredients and how to use them to achieve balanced and layered Indian flavors. Techniques covered include tarka (blooming spices in hot oil), mixing masalas (spice blends), and dry toasting for deeper flavor. I've also provided tips (see page 47) to help you sort through which extra steps will make your food exceptional, and which steps won't make a noticeable difference. Taken together, this section breaks down the components that make up Indian flavor and shows you how to create them in your kitchen.

Hot, Sour, Salt: The Essential Trio

According to Ayurveda, the ancient Indian science of medicine, there are six basic tastes—sweet, sour, salt, hot, bitter, and astringent—and balancing these elements in your diet brings harmony to your being. But according to my grandmother Ambuja, there were three that mattered the most in her kitchen: hot, sour, and salt. Finding balance among these was central to her cooking philosophy: if a dish was off, it was because one of the three was out of sync, and she would fix it by adjusting the other two so they all matched in intensity. I've come to think of them as the three legs of the Indian flavor stool, each relating to, and relying on, the others but also performing a critical function of its own to amplify the overall taste experience of a dish. Here's a closer look at their role in Indian food.

HEAT SOURCES

One of the genius things about Indian food is the way it combines multiple fiery ingredients to create a complex feeling of warmth in your mouth that's alluring and yet hard to pinpoint. Indians and South Asians have constantly refined and adjusted their approach to spicing, eventually replacing the early use of mildly pungent long peppers (*Piper longum*) with the more biting and nuanced black peppercorns (*Piper nigrum*) that started to gain popularity in the twelfth century. The region received a big jolt when Europeans arrived in the sixteenth century bearing incendiary New World chili peppers of the genus *Capsicum*, dramatically changing the cuisine forever. Today, it's normal for a dish to have three or four sources of "fire," such as fresh green chilies (seeds intact), whole dried red chilies, ground red chilies, and ground black pepper. Since no single ingredient should ever dominate a dish, all of them work together to create an interesting and irresistible heat. Here is a way to distinguish the different "heat" ingredients used in this book.

FRESH HEAT

Green serranos are my preference, but green jalapeños and green Thai bird chilies are good substitutes.

DRIED HEAT

These forms of red chili are used throughout: cayenne, ground Kashmiri chili, dried red chili flakes, and whole dried red chilies. Black peppercorns are used freshly ground or coarsely crushed.

SOURING AGENTS

Tangy ingredients add a brightness that counterbalances the heat and deep spice flavors of Indian food. Each region has its own favorite acidic ingredients, ranging from dried sour mango and powdered pomegranate seeds in the north to tropical fruits like kudampuli and kokum in the south. But in this collection of recipes, I've stuck to relatively easy-to-find ingredients like lemons, limes, tamarind, and occasionally vinegar. Tomatoes and yogurt are also used to contribute both acidity and body to a dish. And in the same way different heat sources are employed, multiple sour ingredients are used together, like tomato and tamarind, or yogurt and lemon, adding even more complexity and layers to the cuisine.

SALTED, NEVER SALTY

Salt is absolutely essential in Indian cooking, but salt can also be a minefield from a health perspective. I'm well aware of the public sentiment around sodium levels through my business. I also know from experience that Indian food is pointless without it. Years ago a friend complained that he made a complicated Indian meal that smelled amazing while he cooked it, but was tasteless when he served it. After I prodded him, it turned out that he "doesn't cook with salt." Mystery solved! So while I'm sensitive to those who limit their intake, cooking with little or no salt is a nonstarter with Indian food.

The salt amounts in these recipes have been carefully calibrated. If you use less, you may find yourself underwhelmed by the result. I strongly recommend checking a dish for seasoning just before serving. My father was religious about doing a final taste check, and my first memories of cooking together are of him giving me a spoonful of curry from the pot to taste, to "see if it needs anything." So I encourage you to trust the salt amounts in these recipes, and don't be afraid to make an adjustment at the end to bring out the fullest flavors of the dish.

What Is Tarka?

Tarka (also tadka, chaunk, baghaar, or thaalippu, to name a few) is a term used throughout this book, sometimes as a **first step** to create a flavorful foundation for a dish, other times as a **last step** to add a bold final flourish. The technique is commonly used in South Asian cooking, in which spices and other ingredients are briefly fried in hot oil to release their essence and deliver an elevated version of their flavor to a dish. Tarka involves a sequence of steps to cook each ingredient for the exact right amount of time over fairly high heat. Whether it's a first step or a final one, it's a lively and fun part of Indian cooking, plus it makes your kitchen smell amazing! The drama unfolds with popping noises, an occasional seed jumping out of the pan, and the loud crackle of fresh curry leaves hitting the hot oil. I recommend standing back or having a lid handy when you add your ingredients to the pan.

HOW TO MAKE A TARKA

Choose your vessel

For a first-step tarka, use the pan in which you plan to cook the entire dish. For a last-step tarka, I recommend an 8-inch or 10-inch skillet. Some people prefer saucepans with lids to keep things from jumping out. Or there are long-handled "tarka pans" available through Indian sources (see page 31).

Choose ingredients, line them up, and start cooking

What follows are numerous suggestions that include classic tarka components like whole seeds, dried chilies, and fresh curry leaves, as well as some twists on tradition, like lemon peel and fresh rosemary. Everything is listed below in the order you will add them to the pan, that is, from the longest cook time to the quickest. But you don't have to choose something from each category—even two or three ingredients can provide a flavorful tarka. Simply pick what you like, assemble it next to the stove, and add it in the right sequence. Preparing your mise en place is key because this process moves quickly! The entire tarka can take less than 3 minutes.

NOTE

If you burn your spices while making a tarka, it's best to throw the entire thing out (including the oil), or your dish will taste bitter. Simply wipe out your pan and start over.

1. Oils
Heat until shimmering.
- Recommended neutral-tasting oils with high smoke points: corn, safflower, sunflower, canola
- Flavorful oils with high smoke points: coconut, mustard, ghee
- Avoid these low smoke point oils: extra-virgin olive, walnut, flaxseed, butter

2. Whole spices
Shake the pan as they start to sizzle, pop, and release their fragrance, then add the next ingredient.
- Use whole: mustard seeds, cumin seeds, fennel seeds, nigella seeds, fenugreek seeds, cinnamon stick, whole cloves, cardamom pods, star anise, bay leaf, Panch Phoron (page 226)
- Crush before using: coriander seeds, peppercorns

3. Chilies
Stir briefly for 5 to 10 seconds—they brown quickly.
- Dried: whole dried red chilies, dried red chili flakes
- Fresh (roughly chopped or sliced): serranos, jalapeños, Thai bird chilies

4. Fresh herbs and zest
Beware—these may sputter when added to hot oil due to their moisture content! Swirl the pan as they crackle, then add the next ingredient.
- Herbs: curry leaves, rosemary, sage, thyme, parsley (Note: Delicate herbs like cilantro, dill, chives, and mint may burn in a tarka.)
- Zest: Lemon or lime peel

5. Beans, nuts, and rice
Stir the pan constantly until beans or nuts turn light brown, or cook rice just long enough to puff up and turn opaque.
- For a nutty flavor and texture: white urad dal, chana dal, red lentils, peanuts, shredded coconut
- Uncooked rice adds a little crunch to your dish

6. Aromatics
Sizzle your alliums until they begin to brown and turn fragrant.
- Medium chopped or sliced (minced will burn): any type of onion, shallots, scallions, leeks, garlic, garlic scapes, ginger (cut into matchsticks)

7. Ground spices
Add these at the very end, heat for a few seconds, and remove the pan from the heat to avoid burning.
- Asafetida, turmeric, Kashmiri chili powder

Put It to Use
When your tarka is complete, one of two things will happen:

- *If it's a first-step tarka,* you will continue to build on this flavorful base by adding the other ingredients to the pan.

- *If it's a last-step tarka,* you will tip the entire contents of the skillet into the food you are seasoning, like a saucy vegetable dish, dal, or meat curry. The Indian cook will spoon some of the finished dish back into the tarka skillet and pour it back on the food in order to collect every last bit of tarka goodness from the skillet!

APPLYING THE TARKA TECHNIQUE

Here are some suggestions that include both classic approaches and twists on tradition. My hope is that these ideas get your creative juices flowing so you can come up with your own delicious combinations.

TYPE OF DISH	TYPE OF TARKA	INGREDIENT COMBO SUGGESTIONS
Chicken or meat curry	First step	Neutral oil with mustard seeds, fennel seeds, crushed peppercorns, curry leaves, onions
Dal, classic	Last step	Ghee with mustard seeds, cumin seeds, sliced shallots, asafetida, Kashmiri chili powder
Dumplings or pot stickers	Last step	Neutral oil with sesame seeds, dried red chili flakes, scallions
Feta, whipped on toast	Last step	Neutral oil with mustard seeds, sliced shallots, fresh green chilies
Popcorn	Last step	Ghee, mustard seeds, curry leaves, fresh rosemary
Potatoes, mashed	Last step	Neutral oil with cumin seed, fresh rosemary, sliced garlic scapes (or garlic cloves)
Rice, North Indian	First step, then add raw rice	Ghee with whole cinnamon, clove, cardamom, bay leaf, onion
Rice, South Indian	First step, then add cooked rice	Neutral oil with mustard seeds, dried red chilies, curry leaves, urad dal, onion
Risotto or polenta	Last step	Ghee with fennel seeds, sliced leeks, fresh sage
Seafood	Last step	Coconut oil, mustard seeds, curry leaves
Soup, pureed bean	Last step	Neutral oil with cumin seeds, chopped red onion, dried red chili flakes
Soup, pureed vegetable	Last step	Neutral oil with mustard seeds, cumin seeds, dried red chili flakes, scallions
Steak	Last step	Ghee with crushed peppercorns, sliced garlic, fresh thyme
Vegetables, sautéed	First step	Neutral oil with mustard seeds, cumin seeds, whole dried red chilies, sliced garlic, lemon peel

India has twenty-two official languages, which means there are multiple names for the same concept. Take the process of blooming spices in hot oil: it's known as tarka in Punjabi, chaunk in Hindi, baghaar in Bengali, and thaalippu in Tamil. One of the challenges of writing this book was deciding which term to use. Once chosen, the next issue was how to transliterate (or represent the sound of) that Indian word into English, since different pronunciations exist for the same word across countless Indian dialects. I chose words based on what I found to be commonly accepted terms, and used the most frequently referenced spellings of those terms, but I recognize there are many other valid options.

I use the Punjabi word for tempering spices in oil: *tarka/tadka*. In Punjabi, the *d* is pronounced with a curled (retroflex) tongue, which sounds like a cross between an *r* and a *d*. I found *tarka* to be the spelling that appeared most often in English.

When it comes to the ubiquitous *chili*, Indians are split on spelling it with one *l* or two, but rarely is there an *e* at the end. The number of *l*'s is less about pronunciation and more about personal preference, and both are used regularly. I happen to prefer one *l*.

Dal, the term for split legumes (and the dish cooked with them), is also transliterated dhal, dahl, or daal, perhaps to steer people to correctly rhyme it with "tall," not "gal." All are legitimate, but I chose the simplicity of *dal*.

The terms *pakora* and *bhaji* are both used to refer to fritters made with chickpea flour. Pakora (*opposite*) is more commonly used in the north, while bhaji is preferred in the south. But there is confusion on the topic, because bhaji means something different in Maharashtra (in central India), where it's a vegetable dish, as in pav bhaji, the street food. And northerners use the alternate spelling bhajia to refer to chickpea batter–dipped fritters. This book uses both pakora and bhaji to refer to fritters made with chopped vegetables and chickpea flour.

This varied approach to spelling is a reality of post-colonial India, and it doesn't seem to be changing anytime soon, so we might as well embrace it!

Demystifying Masala

The term *masala* means "mixture of spices" in Hindi, and it refers to the spices that create the backbone of flavor in Indian cooking. Broadly speaking, masalas are dry spice blends or wet pastes. A masala can contain as few as two and as many as a dozen spices. The trick of any masala is that it is greater than the sum of its parts, creating in flavor what instruments do in a symphony.

The most widely recognized masala is garam masala—a ground spice mix used by nearly every household in South Asia. Its ingredients vary across the subcontinent, but the common denominators are the sweet spices cinnamon, clove, and cardamom. It also has the flexibility of being used during the sautéing step, or as a final flourish. I've included a warm-woody one called North Indian Garam Masala (page 222) as well as a more floral version from the south called Kerala Garam Masala (page 224). There are infinite variations on this theme, but these examples show you how one masala can go in two distinctly different directions.

Speaking of regional differences, each part of the subcontinent has its own bespoke blends, like the seed mixture Panch Phoron (page 226) from West Bengal, goda masala from Maharashtra, Chettinad masala from Tamil Nadu, and deeply toasted Ceylon curry powder. In contrast, other masalas are associated with specific dishes, not regions; for example, chai masala, tandoori masala, biriyani masala, and pav bhaji masala. With such an array, Indians make or buy these blends and keep them on hand rather than mix them up each time they need them. Many ideas are contained within the concept of masala, but in all its guises, whether wet or dry, toasted or fresh, it refers to the part, or parts, of a dish that contains the most exciting flavors.

When you use this book, you'll notice the word *masala* is called out in the margin of an ingredient list to highlight the ground spice combination of that particular dish. As you've just learned, there are often multiple masalas in a single recipe, but I chose to highlight the primary spice blend for two reasons: first, so that you can see at a glance how intricate the flavor profile of the dish is, and second, so you can make the blend and have it ready to add all at once. The latter is vital because if you measure spices into a hot skillet one at a time, the first ones may scorch before you get to the last.

I also want you to notice the masala in the recipes so you can see patterns start to emerge and apply these to your everyday cooking—because masalas are flexible and adaptable. Vegetables, for example, often have simple masalas, sometimes just cumin, turmeric, and cayenne. Meat dishes, on the other hand, often use a lot of coriander and have more complex masalas that include cumin, black pepper, cinnamon, clove, and cardamom for depth, and perhaps even a garam masala. I recommend following the Indian custom of keeping the pre-mixed masalas in the "Basics" chapter on hand, which will make it so easy to prepare these recipes and so much fun to experiment on your own!

MIXING YOUR OWN MASALAS

Here are guidelines for spice combinations that complement common foods. This is not the last word on spice blends by any stretch, but they are time-tested pairings that I have encountered over the years and that have been proven to work well. The spices are listed in order of predominance, but refer to the recipes mentioned as a guideline for proportions.

TYPE OF DISH	MASALA SUGGESTIONS
Chickpeas	**Coriander, cumin, Kashmiri chili powder (or cayenne), cinnamon, clove, cardamom** *Chickpeas can handle heavier spicing than dal and are treated like curries in their complexity. Garam masala can be used at the end.* • Used in Tea-Braised Punjabi Chickpeas (page 145)
Dals	**Turmeric, Kashmiri chili powder (or cayenne)** *As the soothing protein source on the plate, dals usually have less spicing than, say, meat curries. They provide a steady source of turmeric in the diet. Sometimes asafetida is included. Garam masala can be used at the end.* • Used in Classic Dal Tarka (page 135)
Poultry	**Coriander, cumin, cayenne, black pepper, turmeric, cinnamon, clove, fennel** *Poultry and coriander have a natural affinity, so it is a primary spice in many chicken masalas. Cinnamon, clove, and cardamom add depth. Garam masala can be used at the end.* • Used in Chicken Chettinad with Black Pepper Coconut Masala (page 151)
Red meat	**Coriander, cumin, cayenne, black pepper, turmeric, cinnamon, clove** *Red meat, like poultry, benefits from lots of coriander and a good dose of cumin. It can handle very bold, layered masalas with lots of sweet, savory, and spicy elements. Garam masala can be used at the end.* • Used in Classic Pork Vindaloo (page 162)
Seafood	**Coriander, turmeric, Kashmiri chili powder, fenugreek, mustard seeds** *Fish masalas range from delicate to zesty and often have coriander as the lead spice.* • Used in Kerala Red Fish Curry (page 177)
Vegetables	**Cumin, turmeric, cayenne** *Simple masalas suffice for many vegetables, and this is the go-to trio for most Indian cooks. Sometimes coriander is included, but it's typically in smaller amounts than cumin.* • Used in Easy Peas Poriyal (page 113)

Toasting Tips

Both tarkas and toasting are wonderful techniques designed to elevate flavor in Indian cooking. In a tarka, the oil-soluble flavor compounds are released into the fat (oil or ghee), which acts as a very effective medium for trapping and distributing them. Used all over India, this approach works especially well for liquid dishes like curries with sauce, dals, or soups.

When we apply dry heat to spices or coconut, we are releasing the volatile compounds into the air as toasty, nutty aromas, which are also nice on the palate but more fleeting. That's why a toasted spice or coconut is often (but not always) added toward the end of cooking. It's also a reason to toast only as much spice as you plan to use quickly, as it loses its potency sooner than untoasted spices. In North India, where there are fewer year-round fresh ingredients to add complexity compared to the south, toasting spices adds extra depth of flavor. In the south, coconut is frequently toasted for a similar effect.

TOASTING COCONUT

TIPS

- If your coconut is shredded medium or fine, the toasting process happens quickly, so keep your eyes on the pan! If your coconut has a coarser texture, it will take a few minutes longer, but still keep your eye on it.
- As with spices, use a nonreactive stainless steel or nonstick pan.
- Use a stirring utensil with a flat edge.

PROCESS

1. Place the coconut in a pan over medium heat.
2. Stir constantly for 2 to 3 minutes—nothing will happen at first, then it goes quickly.
3. Watch for coloring and continue stirring and stirring until all the white disappears and the coconut is almost pecan brown (left).
4. Immediately scrape it onto a plate to stop the browning.

TOASTING SPICES

TIPS

- Use a nonreactive skillet, like stainless steel or nonstick, since cast iron can taint the flavor.
- Toast only whole spices, not ground, which burn too easily.
- If combining multiple spices, make sure they are similarly sized so they toast at the same rate.

PROCESS

1. Place your spices in the pan over medium heat and stir or shake the pan every 10 seconds or so for even browning.
2. After about 3 minutes, you should notice wisps of smoke coming from the spices, at which point they will smell toasty and appear browned.
3. Promptly tip them out of the pan and onto a plate to stop the cooking. Allow them to cool before crushing or grinding.

DO BOTHER TO . . .

Set up your mise en place first. Enjoy the flow of cooking these dishes when everything is prepped and measured, plus it's critical for rapid-sequence tarkas to have your ingredients near the stove within easy reach.

Always rinse your dals first. They get very dusty on their long journey to your cupboard.

Always rinse basmati rice. Removing the starch helps the grains stay separate and delicate.

Put salt in your dal when you cook the beans. I promise it won't make them tough, but it will make them more flavorful (see Dal Done Right, page 132).

Wash your cilantro thoroughly. It grows in sandy soil that tends to cling to the plant.

Freeze your extra coconut milk. Canned coconut milk can be refrigerated but starts to turn after five days, so freeze the unused portion and get another meal out of it. (See page 26 for instructions.)

Find curry leaves. A little challenging, but worth it! Indian and Asian stores carry them, or you can have them delivered overnight—they stay fresh when mailed. (See Sources, page 31.)

Replace your spices every two to three years. I'm convinced spices hold on to a lot of flavor for at least two years, assuming they are kept in airtight containers in a dark, cool place. You definitely know your spice needs replacing if it smells like dust!

Warm plates and serving bowls before filling them. Honor the beautiful meal you just cooked, and don't let it turn ice-cold when it hits the plate. I use my mother's trick of running very hot water over each plate and leaving them stacked in the sink. Dry with a dish towel just before serving. It takes the chill off them without involving your oven.

DON'T BOTHER TO . . .

peel ginger if the skin is smooth. Save yourself the trouble because you won't notice the difference once you've minced or grated it. If the skin is tough, dry, or wrinkled, cut away those parts, but don't worry about removing every little bit of skin.

discard cilantro stems. They have so much flavor! Always chop the stems and leaves together when making Indian food.

wash curry leaves. It makes them deteriorate faster.

seed fresh chilies. Indian food uses the entire chili, so don't throw away those seeds unless you are very sensitive to their effects.

bother freshly grinding all your spices. Pre-ground spices are perfectly fine 95 percent of the time! Occasionally there will be a good reason to do so; otherwise, skip it.

remove garlic's green germ. Its slightly tough texture won't be noticed in Indian cooking.

wash jasmine rice. Unlike basmati, jasmine's texture doesn't benefit from rinsing off the starch, so it's fine to do it, but not necessary.

SNACKS

Indians have perfected the art of making mouthwatering snacks, also known as chaat. In fact, the term *chaat* comes from the Hindi word for "lick," which is exactly what you'll be doing to your fingers when you sample these savory delights. Some of the snacks here evoke India's wonderful street-food tradition, like pakoras with kale and bhaji full of crisp sweet potatoes. They make the act of deep-frying pay dividends, so don't let a fear of frying cause you to miss out on their crunchy rewards! And don't forget to douse all of the above in chutneys from the "Basics" chapter (page 221).

You'll also find some quick and easy snacks of my own invention that light-handedly employ Indian flavors and can be pulled together quickly. Kale chips get a thrilling lift from the tangy chaat masala spice blend (see page 52), a sweet pea dip incorporates Indian herbs and spices (see page 63), and no one can escape the gravitational pull of the Sweet and Spicy Nuts (page 51). The Roasted Tomato Tarka with Yogurt (page 64) comes together easily and creates the most irresistible dip for naan or a baguette. Everyone can find happiness here, whether they're vegan, vegetarian, gluten-free, or omnivore.

SWEET AND SPICY NUTS

Neutral oil, for oiling a baking sheet

SEASONING

MASALA

¾ teaspoon Kerala Garam Masala (page 224)

¼ teaspoon cayenne

½ teaspoon fine sea salt

NUTS

⅓ cup water

¾ cup sugar

¾ cup roasted cashews

½ cup shelled pistachios

¾ cup pecan halves

TIP

Be sure to pay close attention to the timing and cues, so the sugar doesn't burn.

This recipe is so quick to make for something that feels and tastes very special. I like the combination of cashews, pistachios, and pecans, but you could use 2 cups of any type of nut. As they cook, the nuts go through an alchemy that is thrilling to watch: the sugar and water turn to "sand," then melt again into gorgeous caramel. The nuts emerge shiny and crackling, and I can hardly control myself around them!

1. Thoroughly oil a large baking sheet.

2. **Mix the seasoning:** In a small bowl, combine the garam masala, cayenne, and salt. Set aside.

3. **Prepare the nuts:** Mix the water, sugar, and nuts in an 11- to 12-inch heavy-duty skillet. Cook over medium-high heat, stirring constantly with a silicone spatula, until the sugar dissolves and the liquid boils, 2 to 4 minutes.

4. Reduce the heat to medium and continue cooking and stirring until the liquid crystallizes and becomes sandy, about 8 minutes. Soon after the "sand" has appeared, the sugar will begin to liquefy and caramelize—keep stirring for another 4 to 6 minutes, or until almost all the sugar has melted. If you see the caramel turning dark, remove the pan from the heat from time to time, but continue stirring.

5. When the nuts and sugar are mostly caramelized, add the seasoning and stir thoroughly until well combined. Transfer the nuts to the prepared baking sheet, spreading them in an even, single layer as best you can.

6. When the nuts are cool, break up any that are stuck together. Store in an airtight container for up to 2 weeks.

KALE CHIPS WITH CHAAT MASALA

1 bunch curly kale (about 1 pound), stems removed (see Tip)

3 tablespoons neutral oil, plus more if needed

¼ teaspoon chaat masala, or more to taste (see Tip)

TIPS

• To easily strip off the kale leaves, grasp the stem end in one hand; with the other hand encircle the stem with your thumb and forefinger and, in one confident gesture, slide your hand toward the tip, stripping the leaves off as you go. And don't worry about stripping the skinny end of the stem—it's pretty tender.

• Chaat masala is a wonderful funky blend with black salt and sour mango powder, and in India it is used specifically on snacks. It's available at Indian grocery stores and online. Don't have chaat masala? Mix 1 teaspoon fine sea salt with 1 teaspoon ground toasted cumin seeds and sprinkle it on the kale chips. It doesn't replicate the tanginess, but it adds a flavorful salty note.

SERVING

• Serve on the side with Butternut Tarka Soup (page 76).

• Make these for snacking anytime you have a bundle of kale and a warm oven.

Baking kale chips was the first way I got my daughters to eat kale, because it turns out we are all helpless in the presence of crispy, homemade chips—even when made with vegetables! To switch it up, I like to season the kale with bright and tangy chaat masala (see Tips) and serve them as part of an appetizer spread. They are always the first thing to disappear.

1. Preheat the oven to 300°F.

2. Make sure your kale is completely dry by patting it between dish towels (the drier, the better for maximum crispiness). Tear it into bite-size pieces about 2 × 3 inches. Place the torn leaves in a large bowl and drizzle the oil on top. Toss with your hands, rubbing the oil lightly into the kale leaves. If there isn't quite enough oil to moisten all of the kale, add a little more until the leaves are thoroughly oiled. Place the leaves in an even layer on two large baking sheets.

3. Bake the leaves until they begin to turn brown and are no longer floppy, which will take about 15 minutes. If they are still soft, flip them and bake another 2 to 3 minutes to crisp them up. You'll know they're done if they slide around easily when you shake the pan.

4. Remove from the oven and sprinkle with chaat masala—using a small strainer evenly distributes it, but you can also do it by hand. Taste and adjust seasoning to your liking. (Since chaat masala contains salt, no other salt is necessary on these.) Serve at room temperature.

LAMB SCALLION KOFTA

These little meatballs, or kofta, combine the rich flavor of lamb with the brightness of scallion and lemon zest. They are great for passing, either on their own or with a dipping sauce.

KOFTA

1 pound ground lamb

2 scallions (white and green parts), chopped medium (about ¼ cup)

Grated zest of 1 lemon

2 teaspoons minced ginger

½ teaspoon dried red chili flakes

2 teaspoons ground coriander

¾ teaspoon fine sea salt

1 large egg, lightly beaten

½ cup panko or regular bread crumbs

1 tablespoon neutral oil

GARNISH

1 scallion (white and green parts), sliced on the bias

4 or 5 thin wedges of lemon

TIP

Swap the lamb with ground chicken, if you like. You may need another tablespoon of oil to fry.

SERVING

• Pair the kofta with Vibrant Cilantro Chutney (page 229) or your favorite ketchup.

• Stuff this into pitas with chopped cucumber, tomatoes, Pickled Red Onion (page 230), and a drizzle of yogurt.

• Serve as an appetizer alongside Roasted Tomato Tarka with Yogurt (page 64) and warm flatbread.

1. **Make the kofta:** Place all of the kofta ingredients except the oil in a large bowl and mix them together thoroughly (hands work best here). Pinch off about 1 teaspoon of the mixture and cook it in a few drops of oil in a skillet over medium-high heat until it is cooked through. Let cool briefly, then taste for seasoning. Adjust accordingly and proceed to roll the mixture into small balls (a generous 1 inch in diameter) and place them on a plate.

2. Line another plate with paper towels.

3. In a wide frying pan, heat the oil over medium heat until it is hot but not smoking. Add several kofta, being careful not to crowd the pan, and fry, turning regularly, until the meatballs are browned all over, about 7 minutes total. Transfer to the prepared plate.

4. **To garnish:** When all of the kofta are cooked, transfer them to a warmed plate or platter. Shower them with the sliced scallion, squeeze a wedge of lemon on top, and tuck a few more wedges onto the platter. Serve immediately.

CHILI CHEESE TOAST

This spiced-up cheese toastie is inspired by a massively popular snack in India of the same name that is pure, decadent deliciousness. There are many variations, but common themes are green chili, cheese, garlic, and butter, served on classic sandwich bread. Be sure your chilies are fiery hot, and while the gold standard in India is to use Amul, a processed cheese, I prefer a sharp white cheddar. You can, and will want to, make an infinite number of these by increasing the amounts in the recipe. They disappear quickly! (See page 19 for tips on how to test the heat level of your chili.)

CHEESE TOPPING

2 to 3 teaspoons finely chopped serrano or jalapeño

3 scallions (white and green parts), finely chopped (about ⅓ cup)

2 generous cups grated white cheddar

Freshly ground black pepper

GARLIC BUTTER

2 tablespoons salted butter, at room temperature

1 large garlic clove, finely minced (about 2 teaspoons)

TO ASSEMBLE

4 (4 × 4-inch) slices of sandwich bread

Dried red chili flakes, for garnish

TIP

Vegan butter and cheese work well here.

SERVING

• Have these with an icy cold beer or fizzy nonalcoholic drink.

• Serve with a rich tomato soup.

1. Preheat the broiler and set the top rack 4 to 5 inches below the heat.

2. **Mix the cheese topping:** In a medium bowl, combine the green chili, scallions, cheese, and a few grinds of black pepper and mix well. Set aside.

3. **Make the garlic butter:** In a small bowl, combine the soft butter with the garlic and blend well.

4. **Assemble the toasts:** Spread half of the butter equally over one side of each of the 4 slices of bread. Place the bread slices on a baking sheet, buttered-side up, and broil until golden brown, about 2 minutes. Remove from the oven and set the baking sheet on a heatproof surface. Carefully flip the bread and butter the other side with the remaining garlic butter. Divide the cheese and scallion mixture equally among the buttered slices, gently pressing it into the bread, then broil until the cheese is bubbly, about 2 minutes. Remove from the oven, cut each slice diagonally, sprinkle liberally with red chili flakes, and serve immediately.

SWEET POTATO AND ONION BHAJI

1 teaspoon Panch Phoron
(page 226)

1½ cups (150g) chickpea flour
or besan

¼ teaspoon ground turmeric

¼ teaspoon cayenne

1 teaspoon fine sea salt, plus extra
for sprinkling

¾ to 1 cup water

1 large sweet potato, peeled and
coarsely grated (3 cups)

1 medium yellow onion, chopped
into ¼-inch dice (1 cup)

½ cup coarsely chopped cilantro
leaves and tender stems

½ cup neutral oil, for frying

TIP

In place of panch phoron, you can
use ½ teaspoon each cumin seeds
and mustard seeds.

SERVING

Serve with Tangy Tamarind
Chutney (page 233) or lime
wedges.

Bhaji are to South Indians what pakora are to North Indians:
chopped vegetable fritters bound together with a chickpea batter.
Very often they are made solely with sliced onion, but for this recipe
I added sweet potato because I like the interplay between the two
vegetables. A thin chickpea flour batter is all that's needed to hold
them together, so don't be surprised if it seems like a small amount
of batter for the amount of vegetables. Enjoy these for a teatime
snack as Indians do, or nibble on them before dinner.

1.   Crush the panch phoron to a coarse texture in a mortar and
pestle or by using four or five quick pulses in an electric spice
grinder. Transfer to a large bowl and add the chickpea flour,
turmeric, cayenne, and salt. Add ¾ cup of the water and mix to the
consistency of thin pancake batter. Add the sweet potato, onion, and
cilantro and, using two forks, toss together and combine thoroughly.
It will be mostly vegetables. If too stiff, add a tablespoon or two of
water to loosen the mixture.

2.   In an 11- to 12-inch skillet, heat the oil (it should be about ¼ inch
deep) over medium-high heat until shimmering. If you have a
thermometer, heat the oil to 370°F; if you don't, drop a tiny amount
of batter into the oil, and if it immediately bubbles and pops back up,
the oil is hot enough. Line a large baking sheet with several layers of
paper towels or a brown paper bag and set it near the stove.

3.   Give the batter a quick mix and, using a soupspoon, scoop a
rounded spoonful of batter and carefully slide it into the oil. Once
it's in the oil, flatten the bhaji to ¼-inch thickness so it cooks evenly.
Continue to add spoonfuls until the pan is full but not crowded. Fry
the bhaji until golden brown, 1 to 1½ minutes, then flip and cook the
other side about the same amount of time, or until browned. Using
a slotted spoon, transfer them to the prepared baking sheet and
sprinkle with salt. Repeat with the remaining batter, stirring the
batter well between batches.

4.   Transfer to a warm serving platter and serve immediately.
Leftover bhajis will keep for 5 days and can be reheated on a baking
sheet for 5 minutes in a 400°F oven.

CRISPY KALE PAKORAS

In North India, pakoras are crispy chickpea flour fritters that can be quickly whipped together when friends or family drop by, a snack to welcome a visitor. I like curly kale best because its craggy shape holds the batter well, but any type of kale will work fine. Mine are light on batter, heavy on kale, so don't be concerned if the kale doesn't get completely coated.

1. **Prepare the batter:** In a large bowl, combine the chickpea flour, cumin seeds, turmeric, cayenne, salt, baking powder, ginger, and green chili. Whisk in the water, beginning with ¾ cup, to make a thick but pourable batter that coats a spoon. You want the consistency of a thick pancake batter that drops with a "plop-plop" on a griddle.

2. **Add the vegetables:** Fold in the kale and onion and stir very well until the batter gets in the nooks and crannies of the kale. Don't worry if the mixture seems clumpy.

3. Heat the oil in a 3- to 4-quart saucepan or 10-inch kadai to 350°F to 375°F; it should be about 2 inches deep. Line a large baking sheet with several thicknesses of paper towels or a brown paper bag and set it near the stove. If you don't have a thermometer, watch for the surface of the oil to shimmer. You can also check by dropping in a small piece of onion: if it bubbles and pops up to the surface quickly, your oil is hot enough.

4. Give the batter a good stir, then use a soupspoon to scoop a rounded spoonful of the pakora mixture and gently push it into the oil, working carefully to avoid splashing. Repeat, frying 5 or 6 pakora at a time, until they turn golden on the underside, about 1 minute, then carefully flip them with a slotted spoon. Cook until the other side is golden, about another minute. Some of the pakora may break apart, but don't be concerned because the little bits are delicious! With a slotted spoon, transfer the cooked pakoras and any small pieces to the prepared baking sheet and repeat with the remaining batter, stirring it well each time, as the batter will settle on the bottom.

5. When all the pakoras are cooked, transfer them to a platter and either keep them warm in a low oven or serve immediately. Leftover pakoras can keep for 5 days and be reheated on a baking sheet for 5 minutes in a 400°F oven.

Sweet Pea and
Cashew Dip with Mint

Seeded Nimki
Crackers

SEEDED NIMKI CRACKERS

½ cup (70g) all-purpose flour, plus more for dusting

½ cup cornstarch

¼ teaspoon baking soda

1 teaspoon cumin seeds

1 teaspoon white sesame seeds

1 teaspoon nigella seeds

½ teaspoon fine sea salt

6 tablespoons water

3 tablespoons neutral oil, plus more for the baking sheet

TIP

Instead of nigella seeds, you can substitute black sesame seeds. The flavor will be different but delicious.

SERVING

• Serve with the Sweet Pea and Cashew Dip with Mint (opposite) or lemony hummus.

• Break up the crackers and add them to soup.

This snack has many names in India: nimki, namkeen, and namak pare, to name a few. It's the easiest dough—you can make them with your kids—and it rolls out to form crisp strips with hits of whole seed flavor. But unlike the Indian version, mine are baked instead of fried. And they come together quickly, so whip them up for guests, especially if your oven is already hot. *See photograph on page 61.*

1. Preheat the oven to 425°F.

2. In a medium bowl, whisk together the flour, cornstarch, baking soda, cumin, sesame, nigella seeds, and salt. Mix in the water and the oil just until combined without overworking the dough, which should be soft.

3. Place a piece of parchment the size of a large baking sheet on your work surface and dust with flour. Collect the dough into a ball and place it on the parchment. With a lightly dusted rolling pin, roll it out until very thin, about 1/16 inch thick.

4. Cut the dough into 3½ × ½-inch strips (a pizza or pastry cutter works well here) and create a little space between the strips on the parchment paper so they aren't touching. Transfer the parchment to a large baking sheet.

5. Bake in the center of the oven until the crackers are golden, 12 to 14 minutes. When they are completely cool, snap apart any that are attached and either serve or store in an airtight container for up to 1 week.

SWEET PEA AND CASHEW DIP WITH MINT

½ cup raw or roasted cashews

1 cup fresh or frozen peas, thawed if frozen

½ cup mint leaves

½ cup cilantro leaves and tender stems

1 medium garlic clove, roughly chopped

2 teaspoons chopped ginger

½ teaspoon minced serrano, or 1 teaspoon minced jalapeño

½ teaspoon ground coriander

¾ teaspoon fine sea salt

½ teaspoon sugar

2 tablespoons fresh lime juice

¼ to ½ cup water

SERVING

• Serve with Seeded Nimki Crackers (opposite).

• Spread on toast and top with diced tomatoes and flaky sea salt.

• Sprinkle with crumbled feta.

This is a fun dip to make any time of year, but it is especially nice in summer when fresh peas and mint are in season. It is super easy to whiz together and makes a great vegan addition to an appetizer spread. *See photograph on page 60.*

1. In a small saucepan, combine the cashews and enough water to cover them by ½ inch. Bring to a boil, uncovered, then remove from heat. Cover and set aside for 20 minutes while you prep the rest of the ingredients.

2. Drain the cashews, then place them in a food processor or blender (a blender will yield a smoother texture). Add the peas, mint, cilantro, garlic, ginger, green chili, coriander, salt, sugar, lime juice, and ¼ cup of the water. Process for at least 30 seconds, or until the mixture is well pureed. Add more water gradually to thin if necessary. Don't worry if you can't get it as smooth as silk. Adjust the seasoning and refrigerate before serving.

ROASTED TOMATO TARKA WITH YOGURT

Cherry tomatoes have become a wonder of the vegetable world, so sweet and versatile and seemingly always available, thanks to greenhouses and grower efficiency. I love to roast them in the winter, and I found that adding a little tarka on top bumps up the flavor; serving them over tangy cooling yogurt makes them even more special.

1. Preheat the oven to 450°F.

2. **Roast the tomatoes:** Place the tomatoes in a 9 × 9-inch baking dish. Toss with the oil, salt, and pepper and roast until the tomatoes are soft and collapsing, 15 to 20 minutes, depending on their size. Remove from the oven.

3. **Prepare the tarka just prior to serving:** Assemble your prepared and measured ingredients by the stove so they're ready to go. Heat the oil in a small skillet over medium-high heat until it is shimmering. Add the mustard seeds and allow them to pop, occasionally swirling the pan. After they have popped for a few seconds, add the red chili flakes and the scallions and cook, stirring and shaking the pan, until the scallions turn deep golden at the edges, 3 to 5 minutes. Immediately pour the tarka mixture over the tomatoes and stir to combine.

4. **To assemble:** Spread the yogurt in a shallow bowl or on a platter and pour the tomato mixture over the top. Garnish with cilantro and serve immediately.

TOMATOES

1 pint (2 cups) cherry or grape tomatoes (halve lengthwise any larger than 1 inch)

½ teaspoon neutral oil

¼ teaspoon kosher salt

A few grinds of black pepper

TARKA

1 tablespoon neutral oil

¾ teaspoon brown or black mustard seeds

⅛ teaspoon dried red chili flakes

3 scallions (white and green parts), cut in ⅛-inch rounds (about ⅓ cup)

TO ASSEMBLE

¾ cup plain whole milk Greek-style yogurt

1 tablespoon chopped cilantro leaves and tender stems

TIPS

• Use a variety of small tomatoes for a more colorful dish.

• Use 8 to 10 curry leaves, if you have them, in place of scallions.

• Substitute cashew or other nondairy yogurt to make this vegan.

SERVING

• Serve with Garlic Naan (page 194) or warm pita.

• Spoon onto garlic-rubbed toasted baguette, crostini-style.

• It's delicious with roasted lamb and dolmades.

SOUPS

Soups are a perfect place to play with Indian spices and test out the tarka technique. You'll discover how easy it is to season basic vegetable purees with a final flourish of bloomed spices, as in Golden Potato Soup with Frizzled Leeks (page 69) and Butternut Tarka Soup (page 76). And simple spice blends can add depth to the flavor base, as you'll see with Chicken Mulligatawny with Peppery Cashews (page 70), Spiced Chickpea and Vegetable Soup (page 73), and Rasam and Rice Soup (page 79).

Since beans and lentils are right at home in Indian cuisine, they are likewise a star (and good source of protein) in my Spiced Chickpea and Vegetable and Rasam and Rice Soups. And coconut milk brings luscious creaminess to the Sri Lankan–inspired Coconut Noodle Soup (page 75) and others.

There are lots of meat-free options in this chapter that will surprise you with how hearty and satisfying they are. These recipes allow you to use up your farmers' market veggies, too, if that's where you get your produce, though you'll notice that almost all the ingredients here can be found at your local grocery store.

GOLDEN POTATO SOUP WITH FRIZZLED LEEKS

My mother loves Julia Child's recipe for potato leek soup, but she always adds a bit of cayenne "to sharpen the flavor," as she says. I've started taking things a few steps further, mixing in ground coriander and turmeric, and making a ghee-and-leek tarka for an intriguingly bittersweet garnish. I hope Julia would approve, but at least I know my mother does.

2 pounds leeks (about 4 medium), white and pale green parts sliced into thin ⅛-inch rounds (about 5 cups)

TARKA

2 tablespoons ghee, store-bought or homemade (page 232)

Pinch of fine sea salt

SOUP

1 tablespoon ghee, store-bought or homemade (page 232)

MASALA
- 2 teaspoons ground coriander
- ½ teaspoon ground turmeric
- ¼ teaspoon cayenne

1 teaspoon fine sea salt, plus more to taste

1½ pounds Yukon Gold or red jacket potatoes, peeled and coarsely chopped

4 to 5 cups water

2 teaspoons fresh lemon juice

TIP

Easily make this vegan by using neutral oil in place of ghee.

1. Wash the sliced leeks by swirling them around in a bowl of water. Transfer them to a strainer, checking that the water in the bowl is free of any grit, and repeat the process until there is no dirt at the bottom of the bowl. Separate out and reserve 1 cup of the sliced leeks for the tarka and pat them dry so they won't spatter when fried.

2. **Make the tarka:** Line a medium plate with paper towels. In an 8-inch sauté pan, heat the ghee over medium heat. Add the reserved cup of leeks and stir frequently until the leeks are deep golden and crisp, about 6 minutes. Using a slotted spoon, transfer the leeks to the prepared plate; sprinkle with salt and set aside.

3. **Make the soup:** If there's any ghee left in the sauté pan, pour it into a 4-quart saucepan or stockpot. Add the 1 tablespoon ghee along with the remaining leeks and stir over medium heat, sweating the leeks until they are tender and stirring occasionally to be sure they don't brown, 6 to 8 minutes.

4. Add the coriander, turmeric, cayenne, and salt and stir for a few seconds to mellow the spices. Add the potatoes and 3½ cups of the water and bring it all to a boil. Reduce the heat to low and simmer, partially covered, until the vegetables are completely tender, about 30 minutes (this will depend on how small you cut your potatoes).

5. Puree the soup with a stick blender or in a blender until velvety smooth, like heavy cream (you may need to add more water). Check the temperature to make sure it is warm but not blistering hot. Stir in the lemon juice, taste for salt, and divide evenly among four to six bowls. Sprinkle with the leek tarka and serve immediately.

CHICKEN MULLIGATAWNY WITH PEPPERY CASHEWS

My friend Susan Westmoreland shared this recipe with me. Susan and I worked together in midtown Manhattan, just a few short blocks from the Soup Man's tiny shop—the one immortalized by the TV show *Seinfeld*. She and I both loved his unconventional mulligatawny, loaded with nuts and eggplant, and so thick you could almost stand a spoon in it. This is Susan's own wonderful, more traditional version, but it still takes me back to our publishing days and getting scolded by the Soup Man on West Fifty-fifth Street!

SOUP

- 2 tablespoons neutral oil
- 1 large yellow onion, chopped (about 2½ cups)
- 1 large carrot, chopped (about 1 cup)
- 2 celery ribs, chopped (about 1 cup)
- 1 tablespoon minced ginger
- 1 medium garlic clove, chopped (1 teaspoon)
- 1 serrano or jalapeño, split lengthwise, with top intact
- 4 teaspoons Madras curry powder, store-bought or homemade (page 225)
- ¼ teaspoon freshly ground black pepper
- ¼ teaspoon cayenne
- 1 teaspoon fine sea salt
- 1 medium sweet potato, peeled and chopped (about 2 cups)
- 3 fresh or canned plum tomatoes, chopped (about 2 cups)
- 1 cup red lentils (masoor dal), rinsed
- ¼ cup jasmine rice
- 4 cups chicken or vegetable broth
- 4 cups water
- 1 cup canned full-fat coconut milk
- 2 tablespoons fresh lime juice
- ½ cup chopped cilantro leaves and tender stems

CHICKEN

- 1 pound boneless, skinless chicken thighs, trimmed of excess fat
- Kosher salt and freshly ground black pepper
- 1 tablespoon neutral oil

MASALA

1. **Make the soup:** Assemble your prepped and measured ingredients by the stove so they're ready to go. Add the oil to a large stockpot and set it over medium heat. When hot, add the onion, carrot, and celery and stir occasionally until the onion begins to brown, 6 to 8 minutes. Stir in the ginger, garlic, green chili, curry powder, black pepper, cayenne, and salt and cook for 30 seconds, or until the spices lose their raw smell. Add the sweet potato, tomatoes, lentils, rice, broth, and water. Bring to a boil. Reduce the heat to medium-low and simmer, partially covered, until the lentils and vegetables are soft and losing their shape, about 40 minutes, stirring occasionally.

2. **Meanwhile, prepare the chicken:** Pat the chicken dry and season it with ¼ teaspoon each kosher salt and freshly ground black pepper. In a 5- to 6-quart Dutch oven or stockpot, heat the oil over medium heat. Add the chicken and cook the first side about 4 minutes, until browned, then flip and repeat on the other side. Transfer the chicken to a plate and set aside.

3. When cool enough to handle, cut the chicken into ½-inch slivers. Set aside.

recipe and ingredients continue

1 teaspoon neutral oil

½ teaspoon freshly ground black
  pepper

½ cup raw cashew pieces

Fine sea salt

TIP

I prefer chicken thighs to breasts,
as they retain good flavor and
texture and are almost impossible
to overcook.

4.   **Prepare the garnish:** In an 8-inch skillet, heat the oil over
medium heat. Add the black pepper and stir for 15 seconds, or until
fragrant. Add the cashew pieces and stir until golden brown, about
3 minutes. Transfer to a plate and lightly sprinkle with salt.

5.   When the lentils and vegetables are soft, stir in the slivered
chicken, coconut milk, lime juice, and cilantro. Cook until heated
through and taste for salt. Serve the soup in bowls, topped with
peppery cashews.

SPICED CHICKPEA AND VEGETABLE SOUP

MASALA

3 tablespoons neutral oil

1 large onion, finely diced (2 cups)

4½ teaspoons Madras curry powder, store-bought or homemade (page 225)

½ teaspoon ground turmeric

1¼ teaspoons fine sea salt

1 (15-ounce) can chickpeas, drained and rinsed

1 large Yukon Gold or waxy potato, peeled and cut into ¼-inch dice (1 generous cup)

1 large carrot, cut into ¼-inch dice (1 generous cup)

A handful of green beans, trimmed and cut into ¼-inch pieces (about 1 cup)

2 medium tomatoes, chopped into ½-inch dice (2 cups)

2 tablespoons tomato paste

½ cup canned full-fat coconut milk

4 cups water

½ cup chopped cilantro leaves and tender stems, plus extra for garnish

TIP

You can easily swap in other vegetables you have, like cauliflower, celery, sweet potato, or spinach. Just make sure to chop them small so everything cooks at the same rate. You could also use canned tomatoes instead of fresh.

I love this soup because it reminds me of the "soup from a stone" parable: when you think you have nothing on hand, you discover you have the fixings for this delicious soup—fancy that! It's very easy to make and a great way to use up the extra vegetables in your refrigerator, plus it feels so healthy and filling. Serve this with Chili Cheese Toast (page 55) for a perfect weekend lunch.

1. In a 4-quart saucepan or stockpot, heat the oil over medium heat and sauté the onion until soft and very lightly browned, 5 to 8 minutes. Add the curry powder, turmeric, and salt and stir until the spices lose their raw smell, about 1 minute.

2. Add the chickpeas, potatoes, carrots, green beans, tomatoes, tomato paste, coconut milk, and water. Stir well and bring to a boil. Reduce the heat to low and simmer for 20 minutes, or until all the vegetables are tender. If it's too thick, add more water. Stir in the cilantro.

3. Serve in bowls, topped with extra cilantro.

COCONUT NOODLE SOUP

This is a noodle-rich soup with a delicate coconut broth. It's based on a Sri Lankan dish called "string hoppers and sothi" that my grandmother used to make. String hoppers (also known as idiyappam) are freshly extruded rice noodles, sothi is a coconut-shallot sauce, and the combination is delicate and magical. I've transformed my grandmother's dish into a soup by turning the sauce into a flavorful broth and adding the pho-like toppings, so it's a bit of a South–Southeast Asian mash-up. Be sure to have a fork or chopsticks alongside your spoon when you slurp up this one!

SOUP

Kosher salt

1 (14-ounce) can full-fat coconut milk

2 cups water

4 large shallots, thinly sliced crosswise (2 cups)

15 fresh curry leaves (1 inch or longer), thinly sliced crosswise (optional but ideal)

1 to 2 serranos or jalapeños, split lengthwise, with tops intact

¾ teaspoon ground turmeric

¼ teaspoon cayenne

1 teaspoon fine sea salt

5 ounces baby spinach or regular spinach, tough stems removed and discarded, leaves coarsely chopped

1 teaspoon fresh lime juice

8 ounces medium-width rice noodles, such as pad Thai–style

TARKA

1 tablespoon neutral oil

1 teaspoon brown or black mustard seeds

¼ teaspoon dried red chili flakes

TO ASSEMBLE

Bean sprouts

Cilantro leaves and tender stems

Lime wedges

Chili sauce, such as sriracha

TIP

You can remove the green chilies before serving if you're worried about biting into one.

1. Bring a large pot of salted water to a boil to use later for the noodles. Keep it warm as you prepare the rest of the soup.

2. **Make the soup:** In a 4-quart saucepan or stockpot, combine the coconut milk, water, shallots, curry leaves, green chilies, turmeric, cayenne, and salt and simmer over medium-low heat until it thickens to the consistency of light cream, about 10 minutes. Avoid a hard boil or the coconut milk will separate. Stir in the spinach and simmer 3 to 5 minutes, or until wilted. Add the lime juice and remove from the heat.

3. **Make the tarka:** Assemble your prepped and measured ingredients by the stove. In a small skillet, heat the oil over medium-high heat. Add the mustard seeds and allow them to pop, occasionally swirling the pan. After they have popped for a few seconds, add the red chili flakes and sizzle for a few seconds, then pour the entire mixture over the soup and stir it in. Cover and keep warm.

4. **Assemble the soup bowls:** Return the warm water to a rolling boil and add the noodles. Cook until tender, 5 to 7 minutes, then drain and briefly rinse. Divide the noodles among four bowls and spoon the soup equally over the noodles. Top with bean sprouts and cilantro leaves, and serve with lime wedges and chili sauce on the side.

MASALA

BUTTERNUT TARKA SOUP

Elegant and beautiful, this butternut squash puree gets a bright lift from turmeric and cayenne, while the tarka, with the Bengali blend panch phoron, adds little pops of nutty, bittersweet flavors. Sometimes I skip the pumpkin seeds when I'm short on time, but I do really like the toothsome texture they bring to the puree.

ROASTED SQUASH

1 medium butternut squash (2 pounds), peeled and cut into 1-inch squares (6 to 7 cups)

1 tablespoon neutral oil

Kosher salt and freshly ground black pepper

SOUP

2 tablespoons neutral oil

½ large yellow onion, diced (1½ cups)

½ teaspoon ground turmeric

Rounded ¼ teaspoon cayenne

1 teaspoon fine sea salt

4 cups water

PUMPKIN SEED TOPPING

1 teaspoon neutral oil

⅓ cup raw pumpkin seeds

¼ teaspoon Kashmiri chili powder (see Tip)

Fine sea salt

TARKA

1 tablespoon ghee, store-bought or homemade (page 232), or neutral oil

1 tablespoon Panch Phoron (page 226; see Tip)

TIPS

• If you don't have panch phoron, simply substitute 1½ teaspoons each of brown or black mustard seeds and cumin seeds.

• If you don't have Kashmiri chili powder, use a mixture of 3 parts sweet paprika to 1 part cayenne. Make extra and store for future use.

1. Preheat the oven to 425°F.

2. **Roast the squash:** Place the diced squash in a large bowl and toss with the oil and a sprinkle each of salt and black pepper. Spread it out evenly on a large baking sheet and roast until the squash is nearly tender, about 25 minutes, flipping the pieces halfway through. (For the best color in this soup, don't let your roasted squash get too brown.)

3. **Prepare the soup:** When the squash is almost done roasting, heat the oil in a 4- to 6-quart stockpot over medium heat. Add the onion and cook, stirring frequently, until translucent but not golden, about 8 minutes. Add the turmeric, cayenne, and salt and stir until all the ingredients are combined.

4. Add the roasted squash and the water to the pot. Bring to a boil, then reduce the heat to low so the soup is gently simmering. Cook, partially covered, until the squash is completely tender and the flavors have melded, about 20 minutes. Puree the soup with a stick blender or in a blender until velvety smooth, then adjust the seasoning. The soup may be prepared ahead of time to this point, if desired, and rewarmed before serving.

5. **Make the topping:** While the soup is cooking, prepare the pumpkin seeds. Heat an 8-inch skillet over medium heat. Add the oil and pumpkin seeds and stir for a minute or two until the seeds begin to color. Add the Kashmiri chili powder and stir for another minute, until well coated. Sprinkle with salt and transfer to a plate.

6. **Make the tarka:** Wipe out the same small skillet. Add the ghee and set the skillet over medium-high heat. When the oil is shimmering, reduce the heat to medium, add the panch phoron, and cook, stirring constantly, until the seeds start popping and the pale seeds turn golden, about 1 minute. Immediately pour the spices over the soup. Stir and adjust the seasoning. Serve in bowls, topped with the spiced pumpkin seeds.

RASAM AND RICE SOUP

Rasam is a restorative South Indian broth. Sometimes called "pepper water," it features black pepper, a tamarind broth, garlicky asafetida, and bittersweet fenugreek. When served as part of a traditional South Indian meal, it's usually poured over rice, which is lovely, but I decided to put rice into the rasam instead. It makes the soup thicker and more filling than the traditional version, and every bit as peppery and flavorful.

BEANS

¾ cup toor dal or red lentils (masoor dal), rinsed

½ teaspoon ground turmeric

½ teaspoon fine sea salt

3 cups water

SOUP

1½ teaspoons tamarind paste or concentrate

1 large tomato, diced (1½ cups)

½ cup uncooked jasmine or long-grain rice

1 teaspoon fine sea salt

5 cups water

TARKA

2 teaspoons black peppercorns

3 tablespoons neutral oil

1½ teaspoons brown or black mustard seeds

1½ teaspoons cumin seeds

12 to 15 fresh curry leaves (1 inch or longer), thinly sliced chiffonade-style

½ large yellow onion, sliced (1½ cups)

¼ teaspoon dried red chili flakes

¼ teaspoon fenugreek seeds

¼ teaspoon asafetida

TO FINISH

3 to 4 teaspoons fresh lemon juice

2 tablespoons coarsely chopped cilantro leaves and tender stems, plus extra for garnish

TIP

Even though the amounts are small, asafetida and fenugreek seeds will help you attain the authentic taste of rasam.

1. **Make the beans:** In a 4-quart saucepan or stockpot, combine the rinsed dal, turmeric, salt, and water. Bring to a boil, reduce the heat to low, and simmer steadily with the lid slightly ajar (watch that it doesn't boil over). Cook for 40 to 50 minutes (or 20 to 25 for red lentils), or until a piece of dal smooshes when pressed and no whiteness is visible in its core. Stir occasionally while it's cooking, and don't worry if it's a little loose with excess water at the end. This step can be done a few hours ahead of time.

2. **Prepare the soup:** When the dal has finished cooking, add the tamarind, tomato, rice, salt, and water. Bring the mixture to a boil, reduce the heat to low, and simmer until the rice is cooked through and the soup is thick, about 20 minutes.

3. **Make the tarka:** Immediately after adding the rice and other ingredients, prepare the tarka. First, crush the peppercorns with a mortar and pestle to a coarse powder or blitz them with six or seven quick pulses in an electric spice grinder. Assemble all your prepped and measured tarka ingredients by the stove. Heat the oil in a 10-inch sauté pan over medium-high heat. When it shimmers, add the mustard seeds and allow them to pop, occasionally swirling the pan. After they have popped for a few seconds, add the cumin seeds and sizzle for a few seconds. Add the curry leaves, which will crackle loudly, and reduce the heat to medium. Add the onion and sauté for 3 to 4 minutes, until it begins to soften. Next, add the red chili flakes, fenugreek seeds, and asafetida and stir briefly until fragrant, about 30 seconds. Immediately pour the whole mixture into the soup and continue simmering until the rice is cooked through and the flavors have melded, at least 5 minutes.

4. **To finish:** Stir in 3 teaspoons of the lemon juice and the cilantro. If it's too thick, add more water. Taste for seasoning and add more lemon juice and salt to taste as needed. Serve in bowls, topped with extra cilantro.

SALADS

I know many Indians who think of tossed salad as "eating
leaves," which reveals their low opinion of this American
mainstay! But Indian cuisine includes plenty of raw veggie
dishes that are nothing like our fresh green salads, like
kachumbers, tarka salads, and raitas, and I've made sure to
include those here. I have a cucumber and tomato Chopped
Kachumber Salad (page 82) with a sprightly dusting of chaat
masala. Grated raw turnip enjoys a light tarka topping
in White Turnip Tarka Salad (page 85). And the raitas,
those lovely traditional, yogurt-based side dishes, are very
refreshing and such a cool contrast to all the zesty flavors of
an Indian meal that I included two because they're so good!

Other salads in this chapter take a hybrid approach:
Western in form but Indian in flavor. A green salad, a potato
salad, a slaw. And I include a personal favorite, Warm
Chickpea Salad with Cool Lime Cucumbers (page 92), which
is both fresh and filling. Lots of ideas here that can be part of
a summery spread, or simply add some cool crunchiness to
your plate any time of the year.

CHOPPED KACHUMBER SALAD

Kachumber is one of the few true Indian salads. It's similar to Middle Eastern chopped salads, but in this version, the chaat masala gives it a salty-sour note that is distinctly Indian. If you don't have chaat masala, it's still a nice salad: simple, cool, and refreshing on the palate.

SALAD

2 medium tomatoes, chopped into ½-inch dice (2 cups)

1 seedless cucumber, chopped into ½-inch dice (2 cups)

Fine sea salt

1 medium red onion, chopped into ¼-inch dice (1 cup)

1 tablespoon fresh lemon juice

½ teaspoon sugar

TO FINISH

½ teaspoon chaat masala, plus extra for sprinkling (see Tip)

½ cup coarsely chopped cilantro leaves and tender stems, plus extra for garnish

TIP

Chaat masala is a special spice blend sold at Indian stores and online; see Sources on page 31.

SERVING

• Serve with Chicken Tikka Skewers (page 157) and rice.

• Spoon the salad over avocado toast, or tuck it into pita bread with hummus.

1. **Prepare the salad:** Place the chopped tomato and cucumber in a colander set in the sink. Sprinkle lightly with fine sea salt and allow to drain.

2. In a medium bowl, combine the red onion, lemon juice, ½ teaspoon fine sea salt, and the sugar and macerate for about 10 minutes.

3. **To finish:** Just before serving, combine the tomatoes and cucumbers with the onion. Add the chaat masala and cilantro and mix very well—hands work best for this part. Serve immediately, garnished with extra cilantro and with a side of extra chaat masala for sprinkling.

WHITE TURNIP TARKA SALAD

My daughter Anna adores this salad because the combo of sharp turnip and acidic vinegar reminds her of kimchi, her beloved Korean condiment. The inspiration came from the very talented chef and author Monisha Bharadwaj, whose book *The Indian Pantry* I refer to constantly.

SALAD

1 pound white turnips, peeled, trimmed, and coarsely grated (about 3 cups)

¼ cup white vinegar

1 serrano or jalapeño, sliced very thinly crosswise

¼ teaspoon fine sea salt

¼ teaspoon freshly ground black pepper

¼ teaspoon sugar

TARKA

2 tablespoons neutral oil

¾ teaspoon brown or black mustard seeds

¾ teaspoon cumin seeds

½ teaspoon nigella seeds or black sesame seeds

TIPS

• This works with daikon radishes, too.

• It's best if made right before serving.

SERVING

• It's fabulous with Peppery Beef Curry (page 166).

• Add it to a veggie grain bowl.

• Use it anywhere you'd use kimchi.

1. **Prepare the salad:** Place the turnips in a large nonreactive bowl.

2. In a small bowl, whisk together the vinegar, green chili, salt, pepper, and sugar and let sit for 5 minutes to mellow the chili. Pour over the turnips and toss until thoroughly combined.

3. **Make the tarka:** Assemble your measured ingredients by the stove. In a small skillet, heat the oil over medium-high heat. When the oil is shimmering, add the mustard seeds and allow them to pop, occasionally swirling the pan. After they have popped for a few seconds, add the cumin and nigella seeds and swirl the pan a few times while they sizzle, about 10 seconds. Pour the mixture over the turnips and stir well. Serve immediately.

MINTY CUCUMBER RAITA

When your mouth needs cooling down, raita to the rescue! It's actually more effective than water in soothing your taste buds, since the fiery compound in chilies (capsaicin) is oil based and calms down upon contact with dairy. For that reason, I like to offer raita when I'm serving an extra spicy meal. And while not all raitas include the tarka step, I like what tarka does to the flavor and appearance of this classic cucumber version.

SALAD

1 medium cucumber

1 cup plain whole milk yogurt

¼ teaspoon ground cumin

Freshly ground black pepper

Pinch of cayenne

½ teaspoon fine sea salt

¼ cup finely chopped mint leaves

TARKA

1 tablespoon neutral oil

½ teaspoon brown or black mustard seeds

½ teaspoon cumin seeds

5 to 8 fresh curry leaves (1 inch or longer; optional)

TIP

If you have only Greek-style yogurt, you may need to add water at the end depending on the consistency you prefer.

SERVING

• Serve with Classic Pork Vindaloo (page 162) as a cooling side dish.

• It's great with Scented Turmeric Rice (page 187) and Tea-Braised Punjabi Chickpeas (page 145).

1. **Prepare the salad:** Peel the cucumber, remove the seeds, and coarsely grate it on a box grater. Place it in a colander and give it a squeeze to remove some of the excess water. If you like your raita chunkier, you can finely chop your cucumber instead.

2. In a medium serving bowl, combine the cucumber, yogurt, ground cumin, a few grinds of black pepper, the cayenne, salt, and mint and stir well. Cover and set aside in the refrigerator until just prior to serving.

3. Give the raita a stir as the salt may have drawn out some of the cucumber's water. If you like your raita loose, now is the time to stir in a tablespoon or two of water to get the consistency you like.

4. **Make the tarka:** Assemble your measured ingredients by the stove. In a small skillet, heat the oil over medium-high heat. When the oil shimmers, add the mustard seeds and allow them to pop, occasionally swirling the pan. After they have popped for a few seconds, add the cumin seeds, swirl the pan, and sizzle for a few seconds. Add the curry leaves and, when they have crackled for a few seconds, pour the tarka over the raita, stir, and serve.

SWEET AND SPICY CABBAGE SLAW

This simple slaw gets extra zing from green chili, toasted cumin, and nigella seeds. I like that it's so fresh, tangy, and light yet with such a big, happy flavor. It is a perfect contrast to rich meat and poultry dishes and has the distinct advantage of being a great make-ahead dish.

½ large head of white cabbage (1 pound), cored and thinly sliced (6 to 8 cups)

¼ cup sugar

1 teaspoon fine sea salt, plus more to taste

1½ teaspoons cumin seed

¼ cup cider vinegar

2 tablespoons neutral vegetable oil

¼ teaspoon freshly ground black pepper, plus more to taste

1 teaspoon nigella seeds or black sesame seeds

1 large carrot, peeled and grated (generous 1 cup)

½ cup coarsely chopped cilantro leaves and tender stems

1½ teaspoons finely minced serrano, or 2½ teaspoons finely minced jalapeño

SERVING

• Serve this with Grilled Leg of Lamb with Yogurt-Herb Marinade (165) or Chicken Chettinad with Black Pepper Coconut Masala (page 151).

• This also pairs well with Potato Bonda Burgers (page 120) or lamb burgers.

1.   In a large bowl, combine the cabbage, sugar, and salt and mix well. Cover and let sit at room temperature for 20 minutes so the cabbage wilts slightly.

2.   In a small skillet over medium heat, toast the cumin seeds, stirring frequently, until wisps of smoke rise from the pan and they smell toasty, about 2 minutes. Pour the seeds onto a plate to stop the browning.

3.   Drain the cabbage in a colander, then transfer it back to the bowl. Add all the remaining ingredients, including the toasted cumin seeds, and toss well. Adjust the salt and pepper to taste, cover, and refrigerate for at least 15 minutes before serving.

WINTER SALAD WITH SHALLOT TARKA VINAIGRETTE

This is an elegant salad with hints of India in every bite. I call it "winter salad" because oranges are at their loveliest that time of year. Bitter greens—available year-round—are a perfect counterpoint to the sweetness of the fruit and the cashews, and they stand up to the big flavors of the vinaigrette. And while there are a few steps to the method, each is simple and the payoff is totally worth it. You'll want to earmark this vinaigrette and use it on other salads and veggies because it's so delicious!

NUTS

1 tablespoon sugar

⅛ teaspoon cayenne

⅛ teaspoon ground turmeric

Pinch of fine sea salt

¾ cup raw or roasted cashews

TARKA

2 tablespoons neutral oil

1 small shallot, minced (2 tablespoons)

1 small garlic clove, minced (1 teaspoon)

½ teaspoon Madras curry powder, store-bought or homemade (page 225)

1 teaspoon agave or honey

VINAIGRETTE

2 teaspoons Dijon-style mustard

2 tablespoons sherry vinegar

⅛ teaspoon fine sea salt, or to taste

4 tablespoons neutral oil

SALAD

2 or 3 oranges, preferably a mix of blood and Cara Cara oranges

8 cups greens, such as a mix of escarole, radicchio, and endive, cut into ¼-inch-thick slices

4 ounces crumbled feta cheese

1. **Fry the nuts:** Heat an 8-inch skillet over medium heat. Mix the sugar, cayenne, turmeric, and salt in a small bowl. Set a plate near the stove. When the skillet is hot, add the cashews and toss them until they are lightly toasted, about 3 minutes. Sprinkle in the sugar-spice mixture and stir constantly until the sugar caramelizes and the spices are fragrant, 1 to 3 minutes. Tip the nuts onto the plate and let them cool completely. Wipe out the skillet.

2. **Make the tarka:** Assemble your prepped and measured ingredients by the stove. In the same 8-inch skillet, heat the oil over medium heat until it shimmers. Add the shallot, reduce the heat to medium-low, and cook, stirring and shaking the pan constantly, until it begins to turn golden, 2 to 3 minutes. Add the garlic and cook until almost all the shallot is deep golden (but not burnt) and the garlic is pale golden, 1 to 2 minutes. Add the curry powder and stir until fragrant, about 30 seconds. Stir in the agave and set aside to cool slightly.

3. **Mix the vinaigrette:** In a small bowl, whisk together the mustard, vinegar, and salt. Drizzle in the oil while whisking constantly, until the mixture is emulsified. Add the shallot tarka to the vinaigrette and whisk well. Set aside.

TIPS

- If you can't find blood or Cara Cara oranges, navels will work well.
- Omit the feta cheese, and instead sprinkle with 3 tablespoons of nutritional yeast for a vegan version.

SERVING

- Serve with Garlic Naan (page 194) for a stunning first course.
- Pair the salad with flank steak.
- Drizzle the tarka vinaigrette over sautéed green beans, steamed or fried fish, or grilled meats or poultry.

4. **Prepare the oranges:** Slice off the top and bottom of each orange to expose the flesh and create a stable base to stand on. Using a sharp knife and starting at the top, carefully follow the curve of the orange, cutting downward to completely remove the skin and pith. Divide the orange in half lengthwise, then lay each half down and cut it into ¼-inch-thick half-moons. Set aside.

5. Place the greens in a salad bowl and toss with the vinaigrette until completely coated.

6. Divide the greens among six plates. Top each plate with nuts, orange slices, and crumbled feta and serve.

CILANTRO-MINT POTATO SALAD

Potato salad is fun to experiment with since there's so much you can do with it! Here I combine a green chutney-type mixture with mayonnaise. It's a gorgeous, fresh change of pace for all you potato salad lovers. If you like a tangy note in your salad, swap the scallions for pickled red onions. However you serve it, you'll enjoy it.

POTATOES

1½ pounds Yukon Gold or other waxy potatoes

Kosher salt

DRESSING

¼ cup mint leaves

¾ cup roughly chopped cilantro leaves and tender stems

1 medium garlic clove, minced (1 teaspoon)

2 teaspoons minced ginger

1 teaspoon finely chopped serrano, or 1½ teaspoons finely chopped jalapeño

½ teaspoon ground cumin

¼ teaspoon fine sea salt, plus more to taste

¼ teaspoon sugar

2 tablespoons fresh lemon juice, plus more to taste

¼ cup mayonnaise

TO FINISH

3 scallions (white and green parts), thinly sliced on an extreme diagonal (about ⅓ cup), or ½ cup Pickled Red Onion (page 230), coarsely chopped

SERVING

• This is perfect with grilled chicken for a weeknight dinner.

• Make it part of a summer barbecue buffet.

1. **Prepare the potatoes:** Peel the potatoes and cut them into 1-inch chunks. Place them in a 4-quart saucepan and add enough water to cover by an inch. Add kosher salt to taste and bring to a boil over high heat. Reduce the heat to medium-low and simmer for 10 to 15 minutes, or just until tender when pierced with a knife. Drain in a colander and cool completely.

2. **Make the dressing:** Chop the mint and cilantro as finely as possible and place them in a medium bowl. Add all the remaining dressing ingredients and mix well. Taste for salt and lemon and adjust as needed. Set the dressing aside.

3. Just before serving, combine the potatoes and the dressing in a bowl and mix well. Top with the chopped pickled onions and serve.

WARM CHICKPEA SALAD WITH COOL LIME CUCUMBERS

I love the contrast of flavors, textures, and temperatures in this dish: warm, peppery stir-fried chickpeas on a bed of fresh cucumbers, topped with zesty pickled red onion. It's a cross between a vegan entrée and a salad. I even make the chickpea stir-fry part of this dish on its own when I want to turn a can of chickpeas into a quick and tasty dinner. Use the leftover pickled onion on your Potato Bonda Burger (page 120), in Cilantro-Mint Potato Salad (page 91), or in sandwiches or grain bowls.

CHICKPEAS

2 tablespoons neutral vegetable oil

½ large red onion, finely chopped (about 1½ cups)

MASALA

1 teaspoon ground coriander

½ teaspoon ground cumin

¼ teaspoon ground turmeric

⅛ teaspoon cayenne

½ teaspoon coarsely ground black pepper

1 (15-ounce) can chickpeas, rinsed and drained

½ teaspoon fine sea salt

CUCUMBERS

1 large seedless English cucumber, cut into ½-inch cubes

2½ teaspoons fresh lime juice

Fine sea salt

TOPPING

½ cup Pickled Red Onion (page 230), plus extra for serving

SERVING

• Enjoy this as a main dish with toasted naan or pita bread and Radish Raita with Toasted Cumin (page 95).

• Serve as a hearty side dish at a picnic or potluck.

1. **Prepare the chickpeas:** In a 10-inch skillet, heat the oil over medium-high heat. Add the onion and cook, stirring frequently, until lightly browned at the edges, 5 to 8 minutes. Add the coriander, cumin, turmeric, cayenne, and black pepper and cook, stirring constantly, until the spices' aromas soften, about 1 minute. Reduce the heat to medium, add the chickpeas and salt, and cook until the onions are browned, about 5 minutes. Add a little water by the tablespoon if the mixture sticks to the pan. The texture should be somewhere between dry and juicy. Set aside; the dish can be prepared ahead of time up to this point.

2. **Prepare the cucumbers:** In a wide serving bowl, toss the cucumber cubes with 2 teaspoons of the lime juice and a pinch of salt and spread them out over the bottom.

3. Stir the remaining lime juice into the chickpeas and spoon them over the cucumbers, allowing the cucumbers to show around the edges.

4. Distribute the pickled onions over the top and serve with more pickled onions on the side.

RADISH RAITA
WITH TOASTED CUMIN

8 to 10 red radishes

1½ cups plain whole milk yogurt

1 large garlic clove, minced

½ medium red onion, minced
(about ¼ cup)

1 teaspoon minced serrano or
jalapeño

1 teaspoon ground cumin

Pinch of cayenne

Pinch of freshly ground black
pepper

½ teaspoon fine sea salt

TIPS

• Any type of radish will work for
this dish, so use whatever you
find.

• If you have only Greek-style
yogurt, thin it with ¼ cup water.

SERVING

• Serve with Chicken Chettinad with
Black Pepper Coconut Masala
(page 151) and rice.

• Spoon onto a bowl of chili or black
bean soup.

When I see all those beautiful radish varieties at the market, I can't resist them, and it turns out they're stunning in this raita. It's a cooling dish, but the radish adds a hint of sharpness.

1. Trim any stems, leaves, and root ends from the radishes, reserving a few small leaves, if available, for garnish. Rinse the radishes well and pat them dry. Cut 1 of the radishes into matchsticks for garnish and set aside. Grate the remaining radishes on the coarse holes of a box grater; you should have about 1 cup.

2. Place the yogurt in a medium bowl. Add the grated radishes, garlic, onion, green chili, cumin, cayenne, black pepper, and salt and mix everything together. Taste for seasoning and adjust if necessary. Cover and keep refrigerated until ready to serve.

3. Just before serving, give the raita a good stir, then sprinkle it with the radish matchsticks and reserved leaves.

VEGETABLES

We all need inspiration when it comes to vegetables, and the Indian cook has infinite solutions!

The simplest to master is the Indian-style dry sauté, beginning with a lively tarka step to flavor the oil: you add ingredients like mustard seeds, cumin seeds, and fresh curry leaves to hot oil in rapid succession and listen for popping and crackling sounds to let you know they've released their essences. There's never been a better way to season a bag of frozen peas or riced cauliflower!

Firm vegetables like squashes and roots get the braising treatment, as in Butternut Coconut Curry (page 109) and Turnip Coconut Milk Curry (page 115). They both get the tarka treatment, too, but at the end, after cooking, as a finishing touch. Speaking of final flourishes, you'll soon be sprinkling North Indian Garam Masala (page 222) over juicy dishes like Classic Saag with Crispy Paneer (page 110) right before serving, like the Indian cook does, sending the toasty spice fragrance wafting through the air.

Oven-roasted vegetables are not typical on the subcontinent, but my family loves them so much and I found a way to make them Indian: with spices, marinades, and side sauces. All is possible when you reach into the Indian repertoire!

HERBY ROASTED POTATOES

There's a wonderful Indian restaurant in London called Dishoom with a signature dish called Gunpowder Potatoes, which sounds spicy but is actually herb filled and flavor packed. My husband and I fell hard for them the first time we ate there, so this is my spin on that dish. After boiling and then roasting them, I like to rough up the potatoes with a fork to mix in the flavor.

POTATOES

1½ pounds Yukon Gold or other waxy potatoes, peeled and cut into 1½-inch chunks

Kosher salt

1½ tablespoons melted ghee, store-bought or homemade (page 232), or neutral oil

TOASTED SPICE BLEND

½ teaspoon coriander seeds

½ teaspoon cumin seeds

½ teaspoon fennel seeds

HERB MIXTURE

3 scallions (white and green parts), finely chopped (about ⅓ cup)

⅓ cup chopped cilantro leaves and tender stems

¼ cup chopped fresh dill

1 to 2 teaspoons minced serrano, jalapeño, or Thai bird chilies (with seeds), to taste

½ teaspoon fine sea salt

1 tablespoon fresh lime juice

1 tablespoon melted ghee, store-bought or homemade (page 232), or neutral oil

TIPS

• Replace the ghee with neutral oil to make this vegan.

• Resist the temptation to use pre-ground spices here! The toasted, freshly ground spice flavor is part of what makes this dish special.

SERVING

• This goes well with Tandoori Roasted Chicken with Charred Lemon and Onion (page 153).

• Serve with grilled steak and a green salad.

1. Preheat the oven to 500°F.

2. **Prepare the potatoes:** Place the potato chunks in a 3- or 4-quart pot and cover with water by 1 inch. Salt to taste and bring to a boil over high heat. Reduce the heat to medium and simmer for 8 minutes, or until tender when poked with a knife. Drain the potatoes in a colander, then return them to the pot and toss with the ghee until uniformly coated.

3. Transfer the potatoes to a large baking sheet and spread them out in a single layer to allow for even browning. Roast until they turn golden brown, about 10 minutes or more, depending on how browned you like them.

4. **Meanwhile, toast the spices:** Place the coriander, cumin, and fennel seeds in a small skillet over medium heat. Stir frequently and when the seeds begin to brown and smell toasty, in about 2 minutes, tip them from the skillet into the bowl of a mortar and pestle. Let them cool for a few minutes, then grind them to a coarse powder. (Alternatively, use an electric spice grinder and quickly pulse seven to ten times.)

5. **Prepare the herb mixture:** In a serving bowl, place the ground toasted spices, scallions, cilantro, dill, green chili, salt, lime juice, and melted ghee and mix well. Set aside.

6. Remove the potatoes from the oven and, with a fork, press on each potato so it opens to create some good nooks and crannies. Add the potatoes to the bowl with the spice-herb mixture and toss thoroughly. Taste for seasoning and adjust, then serve immediately so they maintain some crispness!

CHARRED CARROTS WITH GINGER YOGURT

My sister, Padma, is our family's queen of roasting vegetables, always drawing the sweetest flavors out of her bountiful central New York farm share. She likes to roast all her veggies until they're nice and dark. I find preheating the baking sheet helps vegetables get a good char on them. In this recipe, that technique also enhances the cumin that coats the carrots. The gingery yogurt is a delicious sauce with just about any roasted or charred vegetable (think beets!).

1. Place a large baking sheet in the oven on the lowest rack and preheat the oven to 500°F.

2. **Prepare the carrots:** In a large bowl, toss the carrots with the oil, cumin, pepper, and salt.

3. Once the oven and baking sheet are hot, remove the pan from the oven and spread the carrots evenly on it. Roast them undisturbed for 15 minutes. Flip them and continue cooking for another 5 to 10 minutes, until tender and charred to your liking.

4. **Meanwhile, make the sauce:** In a small bowl, combine the yogurt, ginger, green chili, cilantro, and salt. Taste and adjust for salt. Set aside.

5. Remove the carrots from the oven and transfer them to a warmed platter. Drizzle with some of the yogurt sauce and serve extra on the side. Sprinkle with cilantro and serve immediately.

CARROTS

1½ pounds carrots, trimmed, peeled, and cut into 3 × ½-inch sticks

1 tablespoon neutral oil

½ teaspoon ground cumin

Several grinds of freshly ground black pepper

½ teaspoon kosher salt

YOGURT SAUCE

⅔ cup plain whole milk Greek-style yogurt

2 teaspoons finely grated ginger (see Tip)

½ teaspoon minced serrano, or 1 teaspoon minced jalapeño

1 tablespoon finely minced cilantro leaves and tender stems, plus extra for garnish

¼ teaspoon fine sea salt, plus more to taste

TIP

For the yogurt sauce, I recommend using a Microplane or ginger grater to get a fine texture without fibers. If you don't have either, mince it as finely as possible.

SERVING

Make this when the oven is already hot—for example, from cooking a roast. While your meat is resting, crank up the heat and cook the carrots.

ROASTED ASPARAGUS WITH TAMARIND AND CRISPY SHALLOTS

Asparagus with tamarind is a winning combo, but it's the fried shallots that make this dish soar. Be sure to cook the shallots until they are nicely caramelized for the full umami effect. When you make this recipe, you'll end up with extra chutney, which you're going to want to drizzle on lots of roasted veggies and meats—plus it keeps for up to 6 months!

ASPARAGUS

2 bunches asparagus (about 2 pounds)

2 teaspoons neutral oil

Kosher salt and freshly ground black pepper

SHALLOT TARKA

1½ tablespoons neutral oil

2 large shallots, thinly sliced crosswise (about 1 cup)

Fine sea salt

¼ cup Tangy Tamarind Chutney (page 233)

TIP

Snap your asparagus as close to the base as possible to get every tender bit of it.

SERVING

• Serve this with a roasted chicken or grilled steak.

• It also makes a nice side dish to accompany pasta or paella.

• Sprinkle chopped hard-boiled eggs or crumbled goat cheese on top.

1. Preheat the oven to 425°F and set the oven rack in the center of the oven.

2. **Prep the asparagus:** Snap off and discard the tough ends of the spears, rinse the spears in a colander, and pat them dry with a dish towel. Set them on a large baking sheet and drizzle with the oil. Season with a little kosher salt and a few grinds of pepper and toss until they are glossy and well coated. (The chutney has salt in it, so go lightly here.)

3. Roast the asparagus spears for 10 to 12 minutes if they are about ½ inch in diameter and up to 20 minutes if they're very thick. Flip them once midway through the roasting time.

4. **Fry the shallots:** While the asparagus is roasting, set a paper towel–lined plate next to the stove. Heat the oil in an 8- to 10-inch skillet over medium heat, add the shallots, and stir them frequently. If the heat is too high, they will brown unevenly, so keep it at medium. Continue stirring until the shallots are a mix of medium brown and dark brown, 3 to 4 minutes. With a slotted spoon, remove the shallots to the prepared plate, lightly sprinkle with fine sea salt, and set aside.

5. When the asparagus is done, arrange it on a warm serving platter, drizzle the tamarind chutney evenly over the spears, and scatter the shallots over the top. Serve immediately.

TANDOORI CAULIFLOWER STEAKS

1 (1½- to 2-pound) head of cauliflower

1 recipe Favorite Tandoori Marinade (page 227)

2 tablespoons melted ghee, store-bought or homemade (page 232), for drizzling

¼ cup coarsely chopped cilantro leaves and tender stems, for garnish

1 lemon, cut into thin wedges, for garnish

TIPS

• Prepare the marinade ahead of time (it can be refrigerated up to 48 hours in advance) so that you can do a quick weeknight roast!

• Use nondairy yogurt in the marinade and omit the ghee to make this dish vegan.

SERVING

Serve with Red Lentil Dal with Spinach (page 142), any raita, and a green salad.

Cauliflower steaks are a perfect candidate for some tandoori love. Everything from their texture and flavor to the beautiful caramelized sunset color tempts. The recipe comes together so easily, and these are such fun to serve, that you'll want to eat them all winter long.

1. Preheat the oven to 450°F and set a rack in the middle of the oven.

2. Remove the leaves and tough base from the cauliflower. Make sure you trim away the base of the leaves and peel as much of the stem's tough outer layer as possible. With a long chef's knife, stabilize the stem of the cauliflower on your cutting board and cut the cauliflower vertically into ½-inch-wide slices. If the head is huge, cut the center pieces in half lengthwise to make them easier to handle. Don't worry if they don't all hold together; just do your best!

3. Line a large baking sheet with parchment and lay the cauliflower steaks and extra pieces on it. With a pastry brush, paint the tops of the steaks and the pieces with half of the marinade. Roast until the cauliflower begins to turn golden at the edges, about 15 minutes.

4. Remove the baking sheet from the oven and carefully flip the slices and any pieces. Brush the remaining marinade all over the cauliflower. Drizzle the pieces with ghee, return to the oven, and continue roasting until the cauliflower is tender when poked with the tip of a sharp knife, 15 to 25 minutes. (If the small bits are getting too dark, remove them.)

5. Carefully transfer the cauliflower to a warm platter, scatter with cilantro, and tuck lemon wedges around the sides. Serve immediately.

GARLICKY TARKA BROCCOLI

I'm not sure about you, but I'm always searching for interesting ways to cook broccoli. I find when I sauté it with garlic, the garlic burns before the broccoli is cooked, so I've started cooking the broccoli first and finishing it with a garlic tarka, and I love the results. While I like this mix of spices and garlic, it's also nice to mix it up with ingredients like lemon peel, scallions, and sesame seeds. Have fun with it!

BROCCOLI

1 tablespoon neutral oil

1½ pounds broccoli, rinsed, trimmed of the central stem, and cut into 1-inch florets

¾ teaspoon fine sea salt

2 tablespoons water

TARKA

2 tablespoons neutral oil

½ teaspoon brown or black mustard seeds

½ teaspoon cumin seeds

½ teaspoon nigella seeds or black sesame seeds

4 garlic cloves, sliced

¼ teaspoon dried red chili flakes

SERVING

• Enjoy with fried rice and your favorite chili crisp.

• Serve next to a zesty red-sauced pasta.

1. **Prepare the broccoli:** Place the oil in a wok or wide skillet over medium-high heat. When the oil is shimmering, add the broccoli florets and stir-fry until heated through, about 2 minutes. When the broccoli is hot, add the salt and water, stir-fry for a few seconds, then reduce the heat to medium. Cover and cook for 3 to 5 minutes, until tender-crisp. Remove from the heat, cover, and set aside.

2. **Make the tarka:** Assemble your prepped and measured ingredients by the stove. In an 8-inch sauté pan, heat the oil over medium-high until shimmering. Add the mustard seeds and allow them to pop, occasionally swirling the pan. After they have popped for a few seconds, add the cumin and nigella seeds and fry until they are fragrant, just a few seconds more. Add the garlic and stir until it begins to turn golden, about 30 seconds. Add the red chili flakes and stir for a few seconds more, then immediately pour the tarka over the broccoli.

3. Transfer the broccoli to a warm serving bowl and serve immediately.

BUTTERNUT COCONUT CURRY

Winter squash and coconut make a luscious pair. They come together deliciously in a dish from Kerala called erissery that is made with pumpkin, mustard seeds, and toasted coconut. This recipe resembles that one, but I like to swirl in coconut milk for extra richness and finish it off with an extra-crispy shallot tarka.

SQUASH

1 medium butternut squash (1½ to 2 pounds), peeled, seeded, and cut into ¾-inch cubes (5 to 6 cups)

1 teaspoon ground cumin

½ teaspoon ground turmeric

¼ teaspoon cayenne

1 teaspoon fine sea salt

1 large garlic clove, minced (1 teaspoon)

1 serrano or jalapeño, split lengthwise, with top intact

1½ cups water

¼ cup dried unsweetened shredded coconut

½ cup canned coconut milk

TARKA

2 tablespoons neutral oil

1 teaspoon brown or black mustard seeds

½ teaspoon cumin seeds

12 to 15 fresh curry leaves (1 inch or longer; optional but ideal)

1 large shallot, thinly sliced crosswise (½ cup)

TIPS

• The coconut toasts *fast*, so keep your eyes on it.

• If you want to add protein to this dish, stir in half a 15-ounce can of rinsed and drained kidney, pinto, or white beans. Beans are a traditional part of this dish.

SERVING

Enjoy with jasmine rice and Gingered Brussels Sprouts (page 119).

1. **Prepare the squash:** Place the squash, cumin, turmeric, cayenne, salt, garlic, and green chili in a wide, deep pan. Add the water and bring it to a boil over medium-high heat. Reduce the heat to low so the liquid is just simmering and cover. Cook, stirring occasionally, until the squash is nearly tender, about 15 minutes.

2. While the squash is cooking, place the dried coconut in a small skillet and set it over medium heat. Don't leave the pan, as the coconut can burn easily. Regularly stir the coconut around until it toasts to a nice deep pecan brown color with little to no white showing, about 5 minutes, then transfer it to a plate to cool. Wipe the pan for use later.

3. When the squash is nearly cooked through, stir in the coconut milk and the toasted coconut and partially mash a few pieces of squash to thicken the sauce. Bring the mixture just to a boil, then remove it from the heat. (If you are preparing this dish ahead of time, set it aside at this point for up to 2 hours, unrefrigerated.) Transfer to a warm serving bowl.

4. **Make the tarka:** In the small skillet you used to toast the coconut, heat the oil over medium-high until it is shimmering. Add the mustard seeds and allow them to pop, occasionally swirling the pan. After they have popped for a few seconds, add the cumin seeds and sizzle for a few seconds. Next, add the curry leaves and swirl the pan; the curry leaves will crackle loudly. After a few seconds, add the shallot, reduce the heat to medium-low, and stir frequently until the shallot is well browned, 2 to 3 minutes. Pour the mixture over the squash and serve immediately.

CLASSIC SAAG
WITH CRISPY PANEER

This dish has a few steps more than most of the recipes in this book, but it's worth the effort. I personally love frying the paneer to make it crispy. I also recommend blanching the spinach before you puree it, because it makes the dish look vibrant. But one shortcut I'm all for is using store-bought paneer, which is now carried at most health food stores (see Tip for alternatives). Since paneer is a dense cow's milk cheese, this dish is your vegetable and protein all in one!

SPINACH

½ cup plain whole-milk yogurt

½ teaspoon cornstarch

Kosher salt

1 pound fresh spinach, tough stems removed, washed

PANEER

1 tablespoon neutral oil

1 (6- to 8-ounce) block store-bought paneer, cut into ¾-inch cubes

TARKA

2 tablespoons neutral oil

1 teaspoon cumin seeds

1 medium yellow onion, chopped medium (1 cup)

3 garlic cloves, thinly sliced

1 tablespoon minced ginger

1 teaspoon minced serrano, or 2 teaspoons minced jalapeño

1 teaspoon ground coriander

1 teaspoon ground cumin

½ teaspoon ground turmeric

¼ teaspoon freshly ground black pepper

¼ teaspoon cayenne

MASALA

1 teaspoon fine sea salt

1½ to 1¾ cups water, plus more as needed

¼ teaspoon North Indian garam masala, store-bought or homemade (page 222)

1 teaspoon fresh lemon juice

1. **Prepare the spinach:** In a small bowl, whisk together the yogurt and the cornstarch. Set aside.

2. Bring a 5-quart pot of salted water to a rolling boil. Set a bowl of ice water next to the stove. Place a colander in the sink. Transfer all the spinach to the pot, submerging the leaves completely for about 45 seconds. Using tongs or a slotted spoon (or both), transfer the spinach to the ice water bath to quickly cool and lock in the color. After a few minutes, transfer the spinach to the colander and press it to remove the excess liquid. There will still be some water in the spinach, which is fine. Set aside.

3. **Fry the paneer:** Heat the oil in a deep 11- to 12-inch skillet over medium-high heat. When the oil is shimmering, add the cubed paneer and cook, stirring occasionally, until the paneer is golden brown and a bit crisp, 3 to 4 minutes. Transfer it and any crispy bits that stick to the pan to a plate.

4. **Make the tarka:** Assemble your prepped and measured ingredients by the stove. To the same skillet you used to fry the paneer, heat the oil over medium-high heat. Add the cumin seeds and, after a few seconds, add the onion and cook, stirring often, until golden brown, 6 to 8 minutes. If there are still some paneer bits on the bottom of the skillet, don't be concerned; scrape them up as you cook the onion.

recipe continues

- If you prefer to use Greek-style yogurt, dilute it with 2 tablespoons of water.
- The small amount of cornstarch prevents the yogurt from separating.
- To substitute frozen for fresh spinach, use one 10-ounce package, thaw it completely, press out the water, and add it in step 5.
- If paneer is not available, you can substitute queso fresco or queso blanco. Note that these are softer and saltier than paneer, so I recommend you stir carefully and reduce the fine sea salt in the sauce to ¾ teaspoon.

SERVING

- Serve with rice and Chopped Kachumber Salad (page 82).
- This is delicious with roasted lamb or beef and couscous.

5. Add the garlic, ginger, and green chili and stir constantly until they lose some of their sharp fragrance and the garlic begins to turn translucent, about 2 minutes. Reduce the heat to medium and add the coriander, cumin, turmeric, black pepper, cayenne, and fine sea salt and cook, stirring constantly, until the spices lose their raw smell, about 1 minute. Add ¼ cup of the water and stir to loosen up the spices and any bits stuck to the bottom of the pan. Add the spinach and stir to combine it well with the other ingredients. Add ¼ cup of the water and continue cooking and stirring until the spices meld with the spinach, about 5 minutes.

6. Transfer the spinach mixture to a food processor, add ½ cup of the water, and pulse until it resembles a coarse pesto. Return it to the skillet over medium heat.

7. Stir the yogurt-cornstarch mixture into the spinach and add the remaining ½ to ¾ cup water to get a consistency that is thick but pourable. Cook until hot, then add the garam masala and lemon juice. Adjust the water if the mixture is very thick. Add the paneer, stirring gently until everything is warmed through, 4 to 5 minutes. (Alternatively, you can serve the paneer on top of the hot spinach for a prettier presentation; just transfer the spinach mixture to a warm serving bowl before you add the paneer.) Serve immediately.

EASY PEAS PORIYAL

1 (10-ounce) bag frozen peas
(2 cups)

TARKA

1½ tablespoons neutral oil

½ teaspoon brown or black
mustard seeds

½ teaspoon cumin seeds

6 to 8 fresh curry leaves (1 inch or
longer; optional)

1 medium shallot, finely chopped
(about ¼ cup)

¼ teaspoon ground turmeric

⅛ teaspoon cayenne

¼ teaspoon fine sea salt

MASALA

TIPS

• You can make this with fresh,
shelled English peas. Just boil
them first in salted water for
4 to 5 minutes, until tender-crisp,
then drain before adding them in
step 3.

• Replace the oil with ghee, store-
bought or homemade (page 232),
for a richer flavor.

SERVING

Serve this anytime you need a
quick green vegetable. It goes with
everything!

This is your answer for what to do with a bag of frozen peas! It uses the South Indian Tamil technique called poriyal, a simple approach to cooking vegetables that starts with a mustard seed tarka, to which you add your main ingredient. After sautéing the mixture, you finish it with ground spices and salt. It's different from neighboring Kerala's thorens (see pages 124 and 125) because it doesn't include a spiced coconut masala. Often Tamils will garnish a poriyal with freshly grated coconut, but since our dried coconut is a little tough, I skip that step and it's still plenty tasty. You could make this with beans, carrots, potatoes, or cabbage.

1.   Remove the peas from the freezer and set them by the stove.

2.   **Make the tarka:** Assemble your prepped and measured ingredients by the stove. In a 10-inch skillet or sauté pan with a lid, heat the oil over medium-high until it shimmers. Add the mustard seeds and allow them to pop, occasionally swirling the pan. After they have popped for a few seconds, add the cumin seeds and let them sizzle for 10 seconds, swirling the pan a few times. Add the curry leaves, which will sputter, then reduce the heat to medium and stir in the shallot, frying it for a minute, until soft.

3.   Stir in the peas, then add the turmeric, cayenne, and salt and mix well. Cover and cook, stirring occasionally, until just cooked through, 4 minutes. Check the seasoning, then place them in a warm serving bowl and serve immediately.

TURNIP COCONUT MILK CURRY

¼ teaspoon fennel seeds

TARKA

2 tablespoons neutral oil

1 teaspoon brown or black mustard seeds

½ large yellow onion, chopped (1½ cups)

1 tablespoon minced garlic

1 to 2 serranos or jalapeños, to taste, split lengthwise, with top intact

MASALA

3 teaspoons ground coriander

1 teaspoon ground cumin

½ teaspoon ground turmeric

¼ teaspoon cayenne

1 medium tomato, chopped medium (1 cup)

1 teaspoon fine sea salt

VEGETABLES

¼ head of white cabbage, sliced thin (3 to 4 cups)

1 large carrot, peeled and cut into ½-inch-thick half-moons

1 pound white turnips (greens reserved, if available), peeled and cut into ¾-inch cubes

½ pound turnip greens, spinach, or Swiss chard, well washed, tough stems removed, coarsely chopped (2 to 3 cups)

¾ cup water

1 (14-ounce) can full-fat coconut milk

1 teaspoon fresh lemon juice

¼ cup chopped fresh cilantro leaves and tender stems

This recipe gives the oft-overlooked white turnip a chance to shine, and it also uses up other humble stalwarts of the veggie drawer, like cabbage, carrots, and hearty leafy greens. It makes a big batch, so it's great for a group, or enjoy it as an excellent leftover.

1. Crush the fennel seeds with a mortar and pestle until coarsely ground. If you don't have one, chop the seeds well with a chef's knife (this quantity is too small for an electric spice grinder).

2. **Make the tarka:** Assemble your prepped and measured ingredients by the stove. In a Dutch oven or 5- to 6-quart pot, heat the oil over medium-high and, when it shimmers, add the mustard seeds and allow them to pop, occasionally swirling the pan. After they have popped for a few seconds, add the onion, garlic, and green chili and stir until the onion is light golden, about 5 minutes.

3. Reduce the heat to medium and add the coriander, cumin, turmeric, cayenne, and crushed fennel seeds. Stir for a minute until the spices lose their raw smell. Add the tomato and salt and sauté until the tomato softens, about 3 minutes.

4. **Add the vegetables:** Put the cabbage, carrot, turnips, and water in the pot. Stir to combine and, when the mixture is heated through, reduce the heat to low and cover for 5 minutes.

5. Uncover, increase the heat to medium-high, and add the greens and coconut milk and bring to a boil. Reduce the heat to low so the coconut milk is simmering gently and cook, partially covered, until the vegetables are tender and the flavors have melded, about 10 minutes. Avoid a hard boil or the coconut milk might separate.

6. Stir in the lemon juice and cilantro and serve.

TIPS

• If your turnips have nice-looking greens attached, definitely use them in this recipe.

• Please resist the urge to use pre-ground fennel! Crushed seeds offer so much more flavor here.

SERVING

• Enjoy this as a stew with some crusty bread or Garlic Naan (page 194).

• Spoon it over brown rice or your favorite steamed grain.

SHREDDED BEETS AND CARROTS WITH SIZZLED GREENS

½ pound beets (about 1 large beet)

½ pound carrots (3 to 4 medium carrots)

TARKA BASE

2 tablespoons neutral oil

1 teaspoon brown or black mustard seeds

½ teaspoon cumin seeds

1 dried red chili, or ⅛ teaspoon dried red chili flakes

1 tablespoon white urad dal or red lentils (masoor dal)

15 to 20 fresh curry leaves (1 inch or longer; optional but ideal)

½ teaspoon fine sea salt

⅓ cup water, plus more if needed

TARKA GARNISH (OPTIONAL)

Greens from a bunch of beets (about ¼ pound)

1 tablespoon neutral oil

¼ teaspoon brown or black mustard seeds

4 or 5 fresh curry leaves (1 inch or longer; optional)

½ shallot, minced (about 3 tablespoons)

Pinch of fine sea salt

This dish uses the same Tamil method of cooking vegetables known as poriyal, described on page 113. It starts with a tarka step that supplies all the flavor the dish needs. I like this vegetable combo because both roots cook at the same rate and are rich in natural sugars, so the result is sweet and tender. And you don't have to make the tarka garnish, but it's a great use of nutritious beet tops, plus it makes the dish even more beautiful.

1. Peel the beets, scrub the carrots, and remove their tops and any stringy ends. Set the beet greens aside, if using. Shred the beets and carrots coarsely with a food processor or box grater. Set aside.

2. **Make the tarka base:** Assemble your measured ingredients by the stove. In a deep nonstick skillet, heat the oil over medium-high heat. When it is shimmering, add the mustard seeds and allow them to pop, occasionally swirling the pan. After they have popped for a few seconds, add the cumin seeds and swirl for a few seconds while they sizzle. Next, add the dried red chili and urad dal and stir briefly until the dal begins to turn beige, then add the curry leaves, which will crackle loudly. Swirl the pan for a few seconds, then add the grated beets, carrots, and salt and stir to combine well. Add the water and stir the mixture until heated through. Reduce the heat to medium-low, cover, and cook until the vegetables are tender but not mushy, 5 to 8 minutes. Continue to check that the skillet doesn't dry out, adding water in 1-tablespoon increments if it does. If there's too much water, remove the lid for the final few minutes of cooking. Set the base aside. (This step can be done an hour ahead; reheat the vegetables over medium heat for 5 minutes before garnishing and serving.)

3. **If desired, make the tarka garnish:** Chop off the stems of the beet greens and discard or save them for stock. Fold the big leaves in half lengthwise and slice out the center stem. Chop the greens into roughly 1-inch pieces to yield about 2 cups, then wash and pat them dry. Set aside.

- You can make this with all beets or all carrots if you like.
- If you don't have beet greens, you can substitute about 2 cups of chopped Swiss chard or mustard greens.

SERVING

- Serve with rice and Comforting Chickpeas and Potatoes (page 146) for a perfect vegan dinner.
- Serve with chicken and Scented Turmeric Rice (page 187).

4. Have your prepped and measured tarka ingredients by the stove. In a medium 10-inch skillet, heat the oil over medium-high heat. When it is hot, add the mustard seeds and allow them to pop, occasionally swirling the pan. After they have popped for a few seconds, add the curry leaves, wait a few seconds while they crackle, then add the shallots and sauté, stirring constantly, until soft, about a minute. Add the beet greens and salt and stir-fry until the greens are lightly cooked, 1 to 2 minutes.

5. Spoon the beets and carrots into a warm serving bowl and arrange the greens (if using) on top of the vegetables. Serve immediately.

GINGERED BRUSSELS SPROUTS

Turmeric and cayenne are two spices found in most Indian vegetable dishes, and in some cases they may be the only ground spices used. The turmeric brings brightness, cayenne adds a gentle kick, and salt rounds out the equation. I use that stripped-down approach for spicing Brussels sprouts here, with the additional interest of fried ginger matchsticks.

1½ pounds Brussels sprouts

3 tablespoons neutral oil

1 (1½-inch) piece of ginger (about 1 inch in diameter), cut into matchsticks (¼ cup)

¼ teaspoon ground turmeric

⅛ teaspoon cayenne

½ teaspoon fine sea salt

2 tablespoons water

1 teaspoon fresh lemon juice

MASALA

TIPS

• Don't bother peeling the ginger, but do slice off any tough bits or dried-out ends.

• To make matchsticks, cut the ginger lengthwise into very thin slabs, then stack the slabs and cut them lengthwise again into slivers.

SERVING

• This dish has a mild flavor, so serve it with fish, chicken, or tofu.

• Add these to a grain bowl.

1. Trim the base of the Brussels sprouts and any wilted or damaged outer leaves, then quarter them lengthwise. If some are extra large or extra small, adjust your cuts so all the pieces are roughly the same size and will cook at the same rate. Rinse, drain, and set aside.

2. In a 12-inch nonstick skillet, heat 1 tablespoon of the oil over medium heat. Add the ginger matchsticks and fry until fragrant and beginning to brown and turn crisp, 1 to 2 minutes. Using a slotted spoon, transfer the ginger pieces to a small bowl and set aside.

3. Heat the remaining 2 tablespoons oil in the skillet over medium-high heat. Stir in the Brussels sprouts and toss well, then add the turmeric, cayenne, salt, and water and stir, turning the sprouts to evenly distribute the spices. Cover the pan, reduce the heat to medium-low, and cook, stirring periodically, until the sprouts are nearly tender when pierced with a sharp knife, 10 to 12 minutes, depending on their size. Remove the lid, increase the heat to high, and stir the sprouts while shaking the pan until all the water has evaporated and they are golden, about 2 minutes. Remove from the heat and stir in the lemon juice. Transfer to a warm serving dish and sprinkle with ginger matchsticks. Serve immediately.

POTATO BONDA BURGERS

This is a veggie burger for carb lovers! It takes two Indian potato snacks, aloo tikki and bonda, and combines them into one satisfying potato patty, studded with onion, urad dal, mustard seeds, and cashews. Eat them as burgers or serve them as sliders, your choice. Either way, I guarantee you'll be delighted at how satisfying they are, especially when you load on the flavorful condiments!

POTATOES

2 large russet potatoes
(1½ pounds), peeled and cut
into 1-inch chunks

Kosher salt

TARKA

2 tablespoons neutral oil, plus
½ cup or more for frying the
burgers

1¼ teaspoons brown or black
mustard seeds

2 teaspoons white urad dal or red
lentils (masoor dal)

½ large yellow onion, finely
chopped (1½ cups)

3 teaspoons minced ginger

1½ teaspoons minced serrano,
or 3 teaspoons minced jalapeño

MASALA ⎰ Generous ¼ teaspoon ground
turmeric

¼ teaspoon cayenne

1 teaspoon fine sea salt

½ cup panko or regular bread
crumbs

1 large egg, lightly beaten

⅓ cup broken cashew pieces
(raw or roasted)

TO ASSEMBLE

2 tablespoons salted butter, at
room temperature

6 brioche burger buns, or 10 slider
buns, such as King's Hawaiian
Savory Butter Rolls

2 plum tomatoes, thinly sliced

Pickled Red Onion (page 230) or
sliced red onion

Lettuce leaves

Condiments of your choice (see Tip)

1. **Prepare the potatoes:** Place the potatoes in a 4-quart saucepan with enough salted water to cover them by 1 inch and bring to a boil. Reduce the heat to medium and continue boiling until tender when pierced with a sharp knife, 8 to 9 minutes. Drain and transfer the potatoes to a medium bowl and mash them coarsely with a potato masher, leaving some small chunks for texture. Set aside.

2. **Make the tarka:** Assemble your prepped and measured ingredients by the stove. In a 12-inch cast-iron or nonstick skillet, heat 2 tablespoons of the oil over medium-high heat. When the oil shimmers, add the mustard seeds and allow them to pop for a few seconds, occasionally swirling the pan. After they have popped for a few seconds, add the urad dal and fry for a few seconds until it barely begins to color. Next, add the onion and stir frequently until it turns light brown, 3 to 5 minutes. Add the ginger, green chili, turmeric, cayenne, and sea salt and sauté until fragrant, 1 to 2 minutes. Pour the mixture into the potatoes and mix together thoroughly. Wipe the skillet clean and set aside.

3. Add the panko, egg, and cashews to the potatoes and stir with a fork until well combined. When the potato mixture is cool enough, form it into ½-inch-thick, 3-inch-wide patties and set them on a large plate. (These can be covered and refrigerated for up to 1 day.)

4. Preheat the oven to 350°F.

TIP

Make these vegan by using an egg substitute and vegan butter and buns.

SERVING

• Try these with Vibrant Cilantro Chutney (page 229), spicy ketchup, or chili sauce mixed with mayonnaise.
• These make a great lunch alongside Sweet and Spicy Cabbage Slaw (page 87) or White Turnip Tarka Salad (page 85).

5.   Line a plate with paper towels or a brown paper bag. Add the remaining ½ cup oil, or enough to provide ¼ inch depth, in the 12-inch skillet used before, and set over medium-high heat. When the oil is shimmering, slip a batch of the patties in without crowding them and fry until well browned, about 4 minutes. Using two spatulas, flip them carefully and fry the other side until browned, about 4 minutes more. Transfer to the prepared plate and repeat with the remaining patties.

6.   **Assemble the burgers:** Butter the cut sides of the buns. Fit them on a large baking sheet, buttered-side down, and bake until lightly browned, about 7 minutes.

7.   Place each bonda burger on a bun and serve with a platter of sliced tomato, red onion, lettuce leaves, and condiments for topping.

CABBAGE AND PEPPERS WITH CRUNCHY DAL

Need ideas for winter cabbage? Look no further, because this dish is delicately seasoned, easy, and very tasty. It's another vegetable in the South Indian poriyal style that I mentioned on page 113, so it's a dryish sauté in which white urad dal is actually treated like a spice and sautéed along with mustard seeds and curry leaves. The urad dal adds a pleasantly nutty taste and crunchy texture to the meltingly soft vegetables in this dish.

VEGETABLES

½ medium head of white cabbage (1 to 1¼ pounds)

1 red bell pepper, seeded, ribs removed

TARKA

2 tablespoons neutral oil

1 teaspoon brown or black mustard seeds

12 to 15 fresh curry leaves (1 inch or longer; optional, but ideal)

1 tablespoon white urad dal or red lentils (masoor dal)

1 medium yellow onion, finely chopped (about 1 cup)

3 garlic cloves, gently crushed with the side of a knife

2 serranos or small jalapeños, split lengthwise, tops intact

½ teaspoon ground turmeric

½ teaspoon fine sea salt

3 tablespoons chopped cilantro leaves and tender stems

TIPS

• White or green cabbage works best here for color and texture. I don't recommend napa cabbage because it makes the dish too watery.

• Urad dal can be purchased at an Indian grocery or online. Split red lentils can be substituted for texture but won't give you the same nutty flavor as urad dal.

SERVING

Serve topped with seared tofu and a sriracha-style chili sauce.

1. **Prepare the vegetables:** Finely slice the cabbage on the thin (⅛-inch) slicing blade of a food processor or with a sharp knife (you'll have 10 to 12 cups). Finely slice the bell pepper and set it aside with the cabbage.

2. **Make the tarka:** Assemble all your prepped and measured ingredients by the stove. In a wok or 12-inch nonstick pan, heat the oil over medium-high heat until it shimmers, then add the mustard seeds and allow them to pop, occasionally swirling the pan. After they have popped for a few seconds, add the curry leaves, which will crackle loudly, then quickly add the urad dal and stir until they begin to turn beige—this happens fast. Immediately add the onion, garlic, and green chilies and sauté until the onion is tender, 2 to 3 minutes.

3. Add the turmeric, salt, and the sliced cabbage and bell pepper and mix well. Cover and reduce the heat to medium-low. Cook, stirring occasionally, until the vegetables are softened, 5 to 8 minutes. Uncover, increase the heat to medium-high, and stir until any excess moisture evaporates; this dish should have no excess liquid. Discard the garlic cloves and green chilies before serving, if desired. Remove from the heat, stir in the cilantro, and serve warm.

GREEN BEAN, CORN, AND COCONUT THOREN

Thoren is the Kerala cook's go-to method for sautéing vegetables. Similar to the Tamil poriyal (see page 113), it begins with a mustard-seed tarka to which chopped or shredded vegetables are added. The trademark of thoren is the final addition of a lightly spiced coconut paste. The seasoning is gentle because the focus is on the tender-crisp texture of the vegetables that is enhanced by coconut. When corn is in season, I like to combine it with green beans, but in Kerala, it is often made with just green beans or shredded cabbage, both of which are also delicious! *See photograph on page 126.*

VEGETABLES

12 ounces fresh green beans

1½ cups fresh or frozen corn kernels

SPICED COCONUT

⅔ cup dried unsweetened shredded coconut

MASALA

¾ teaspoon ground cumin

½ teaspoon ground coriander

¼ teaspoon ground turmeric

⅛ teaspoon cayenne

1 serrano or jalapeño, split lengthwise, top intact

2 medium garlic cloves, gently crushed with the side of a knife

1 teaspoon fine sea salt

¼ to ½ cup water

TARKA

2 tablespoons neutral oil

1 teaspoon brown or black mustard seeds

1 small dried red chili, or ⅛ teaspoon dried red pepper flakes

20 fresh curry leaves (1 inch or longer; optional)

1 tablespoon uncooked jasmine or basmati rice

TIPS

• It's essential to cut the green beans as small as the corn kernels for this dish to come out right.

• Adding uncooked rice to the tarka adds an extra bit of texture.

SERVING

The mild flavors of this dish go well with chicken or fish.

1. **Prepare the vegetables:** Trim the beans and chop them into very small ¼-inch lengths (the small size allows the coconut and spices to stick to the beans). It helps to line up 6 to 8 beans at a time and cut them together. If using frozen corn, place it in a colander and run cool water over it until it thaws; drain well.

2. **Make the spiced coconut:** In a small bowl and using a spoon, mix together the coconut, cumin, coriander, turmeric, cayenne, green chili, crushed garlic, and salt with ¼ cup of the water, or enough to make a moist mixture that sticks together—it should not be watery. Set aside.

3. **Begin the tarka:** The following steps are done in rapid sequence, so have your prepped and measured ingredients by the stove. In a wok or large frying pan, heat the oil over medium-high heat until it shimmers. Add the mustard seeds and allow them to pop, occasionally swirling the pan. After they have popped for a few seconds, add the dried red chili and let it sizzle for a few seconds, then quickly add the curry leaves and let them sputter for a few more seconds. Add the rice, which will turn puffy and opaque in a few seconds. Promptly add the beans and corn, reduce the heat to medium, and stir frequently until the vegetables begin to turn tender and the beans take on a brighter green color, about 5 minutes.

4. Stir in the coconut mixture and continue cooking until the vegetables are fully cooked but still have a slight crispness, about 5 minutes more. Remove the garlic cloves and fresh green and dried red chilies before serving, if you like. Taste for salt and serve immediately.

RICED CAULIFLOWER THOREN

Thoren was one of the first dishes I ever learned to cook, but only recently have I started applying the method to riced cauliflower. As I outlined on the previoius page, thoren is a tarka-based sauté with subtle spicing, and cauliflower is a natural candidate for this approach because a few seasonings can transform it from something bland and plain into a flavorful side dish. And now you can easily find riced cauliflower in the freezer section of grocery stores, though it's also easy to make at home. *See photograph on page 127.*

MASALA

1 medium head of cauliflower (1½ pounds), trimmed of all leaves

SPICED COCONUT

½ cup dried unsweetened shredded coconut

1 teaspoon ground coriander

½ teaspoon ground turmeric

1 teaspoon fine sea salt

TARKA

2 tablespoons neutral oil

1 teaspoon brown or black mustard seeds

1 teaspoon cumin seeds

1 small dried red chili, or ⅛ teaspoon dried red chili flakes

12 fresh curry leaves (1 inch or longer; optional)

1 medium yellow onion, finely chopped (1 cup)

2 tablespoons chopped cilantro leaves and tender stems, for garnish

TIP

• If you don't have a food processor, you can grate the cauliflower on a box grater, or substitute a 10-ounce package of frozen riced cauliflower. Be sure to defrost and drain it thoroughly before cooking.

SERVING

• Serve with Tandoori Roasted Chicken with Charred Lemon and Onion (page 153) for some low-carb deliciousness.

• Have with fish and Butternut Coconut Curry (page 109).

1. Cut the cauliflower in half through the stem, remove (and discard) the firm core, and cut the head into florets. Place a third of the florets in a food processor and process until the pieces are about the size of (or smaller than) a peppercorn. Transfer it to a large bowl and repeat two more times.

2. **Make the spiced coconut:** In a small bowl, combine the coconut, coriander, turmeric, and salt and set aside. (No water is needed because the cauliflower gives up a lot of moisture.)

3. **Make the tarka:** Assemble your prepped and measured ingredients by the stove. In a deep 11- to 12-inch sauté pan or wok with a lid, heat the oil over medium-high heat until it shimmers. When hot, add the mustard seeds and allow them to pop for a few seconds, occasionally swirling the pan. After they have popped for a few seconds, add the cumin seeds and give them a few seconds to sizzle, swirling the pan a few times. Next, add the red chili and cook for a few seconds, then toss in the curry leaves. After they crackle for a few seconds, add the onion and sauté until the edges turn brown, 4 to 5 minutes.

4. Add all the cauliflower and stir to combine completely. Reduce the heat to low, cover, and cook for 6 to 8 minutes, until the cauliflower is tender, stirring occasionally. Remove the lid, increase the heat to medium-high, and add the spiced coconut. Stir for another 2 to 3 minutes to meld the flavors and evaporate any water. Remove from heat. Garnish with cilantro and serve immediately.

Green Bean, Corn,
and Coconut Thoren

Riced Cauliflower
Thoren

ROOT VEGETABLE MASH WITH SHALLOT TARKA

In the wintertime, I always have more roots and tubers than I know what to do with. If you find yourself in the same predicament, try this dish. It takes those veggies to the next level, with a delightful curry leaf and browned shallot tarka. Using potatoes gives this a nice creamy texture, but you could also use all root vegetables like parsnips, turnips, and carrots instead.

VEGETABLES

1 pound parsnips

1 pound Yukon Gold or sweet potatoes

Kosher salt

TARKA

3 tablespoons unrefined coconut oil or neutral oil

1 teaspoon brown or black mustard seeds

1 dried red chili, or ⅛ teaspoon dried red chili flakes

10 fresh curry leaves (1 inch or longer; optional but ideal)

1 large shallot, thinly sliced crosswise (½ cup)

1 serrano or jalapeño, cut crosswise into 3 or 4 sections (optional; see Tip)

½ teaspoon fine sea salt

A few grinds of black pepper

TIP

You'll cut the fresh chili into sections to let some of the seeds out, but not so many that it overwhelms the gentleness of this dish.

SERVING

• Enjoy this with slow-braised meats like short ribs or lamb shanks.

• Serve it as a flavorful vegan alternative to mashed potatoes.

1. **Prepare the vegetables:** Peel the parsnips and potatoes and dice them into 1-inch cubes. Place them in a saucepan and cover with water by an inch. Add kosher salt to taste and bring to a boil. Reduce the heat to medium-low and continue to boil for 10 to 15 minutes, or until tender. Drain the vegetables in a colander, then return them to the saucepan. While still hot, mash them but leave the mixture chunky. Cover and set aside. (The vegetables can be prepared up to this point as much as a day ahead and reheated just before serving.)

2. **Make the tarka:** Assemble your prepped and measured ingredients by the stove. Heat the coconut oil in a small skillet over medium-high heat. Add the mustard seeds and allow them to pop, occasionally swirling the pan. After they have popped for a few seconds, add the dried red chili and fry for a few seconds. Next, drop in the curry leaves, which will crackle and turn crisp, then add the shallots and green chili (if using) and stir until the shallots turn light brown, about 3 minutes. Add the sea salt and black pepper and stir briefly. Remove from the heat.

3. Check that the mash is nice and hot (warm over medium-low heat if needed) and, if it seems dry, add a bit of hot water to moisten it to the consistency of chunky mashed potatoes. Reserve a few fried curry leaves for garnish, then pour the hot tarka mixture over the mash and stir to combine. Transfer to a warm serving dish and arrange the reserved curry leaves on top.

DALS AND CHICKPEAS

Dal is a central part of the Indian diet, especially for vegetarians. Its name comes from the Sanskrit word meaning "to split or break open" and is used broadly to refer to raw split legumes, lentils, and beans (all of them pulses), as well as to the finished dish made with them. Split, skinned legumes cook faster and are more digestible and therefore more nourishing than whole beans with intact casings. South Asians eat this health-giving food at least once a day, usually over rice. And it's an ideal solution if you're looking for plant-based sources of protein. Dal is also a perfect blank canvas that takes beautifully to the tarka treatment and loves to be enriched with ghee, cream, or coconut. There are so many wonderful traditional approaches, it was hard to narrow them down for this book, but I landed on these five dal recipes that feature a variety of beans and a range of regional styles. There is, however, a small learning curve with cooking dal, so definitely refer to Dal Done Right on page 132 if you aren't already familiar with preparing dal. Whether you like the stovetop method or an electric pressure cooker (such as an Instant Pot), my recipes and tips will see you through.

Chickpeas (chanas) are another great source of protein eaten in India, taking on myriad flavors, textures, and forms across the subcontinent. Like dal, chickpeas also fit in perfectly with today's search for easy-to-prepare nonmeat proteins. When I think of chanas, I think "comfort food," and I've included two very cozy options.

For such a basic dish, there's a surprising amount to know about cooking dal! And just to keep things interesting, dals (legumes and beans) come in many forms—split, whole, skin on, skin off (hulled)—and each one cooks a little differently. All the options can be dizzying, but remain calm because each of my recipes clearly states which dal you need as well as a good alternative. For those who have an electric pressure cooker (such as an Instant Pot), I provide water ratios and times so that you can cook the beans more quickly. However, all the recipes are geared toward the stovetop method in order to be more universally usable. These tips will guide you through the process so you can cook with confidence—and love the results.

RINSING

Do rinse your dal before cooking to remove dust and any debris. If you don't, an unappealing foam will collect on top when it boils (see Skimming, below). To rinse it, simply place the dal in either the pot you plan to cook it in or a large bowl. Fill the vessel with water and swish it around with your hand. If the water is very cloudy, repeat the process, then pour off all the water and proceed with the recipe. (No need to drain every drop; the end result will be soupy so a little extra water doesn't matter.)

SKIP SOAKING

It may cut down the final cooking time by a few minutes, but the beans are small so the difference won't be that significant.

SALTING

To salt or not to salt the beans during the first cook: This is a controversial topic! From a scientific and flavor standpoint, I'm with the school that believes in adding part of the salt to the cooking water and the remaining salt to the flavor base. The dish will have a fuller flavor if the salt permeates the beans from the start.

COOKING

Stovetop or electric pressure cooker? Don't worry, I have instructions for both! If you're using the stovetop method, you'll need to keep a watchful eye. It's totally normal for dal to bubble over or dry out, so be prepared to check it a lot and add water as needed—which is exactly why people like to use an electric pressure cooker; it removes the variables as well as speeds up the process. It also keeps your stove free from yet another pot. Note that the natural release time for an electric pressure cooker is approximately 15 minutes.

SKIMMING

If you're doing the stovetop method and you see a thick foam collecting on top, skim it off. It's nothing bad, just some impurities rising to the surface.

TIMING

I provide guidelines, but don't be surprised if your beans need more time if you're using the stovetop method. Some beans are just plain stubborn, so don't worry that you did something wrong!

SEASONING

This is the second phase of cooking, which involves creating a flavor base that will be added to the cooked beans and simmered together to meld the flavors. Prep this while the dal is cooking.

FINISHING

As the final touch, you might drizzle your dal with a tarka, add a squeeze of lemon, or sprinkle in some garam masala. You can do this in the pot or in the serving dish, you decide. Now enjoy!

DAL COOK TIMES

This chart allows you to see cooking times for the stovetop and for electric pressure cookers at a glance. If a recipe calls for a combination of dals simmered together, always use the longest cook time. Some factors that might affect these times include the age of your beans; whether you like chunky (less time) versus smooth dal (more time); and an increased volume of beans (more time needed). Also note that these times assume *no soaking*, because it's not essential for these beans. But if you do soak your dal, it will shorten the cook time.

DAL TYPE	STOVETOP WATER RATIO*	STOVETOP TIME	ELECTRIC PRESSURE COOKER WATER RATIO*	ELECTRIC PRESSURE COOKER TIME
Black Lentils (beluga)	1:3	35 minutes	1:3	15 minutes
Black Urad Dal	1:3	40 to 50 minutes	1:3	20 minutes
Chana Dal	1:4	60 to 75 minutes	1:3	35 minutes
Red Lentils (masoor dal)	1:4	25 minutes	1:3	5 minutes
Toor Dal	1:3½	40 to 50 minutes	1:3	10 minutes
Yellow Moong Dal	1:4	25 to 35 minutes	1:3	5 minutes
Yellow Split Peas	1:4	40 to 50 minutes	1:3	20 minutes

* Ratios represent dal to water

CLASSIC DAL TARKA

Also spelled dal tadka, this is a perfect example of Indians turning basic legumes into something thrilling. It includes two tarkas, one to bolster the flavor of the simmered beans and a second that serves as a supercharged garnish. Ghee will give this dish extra depth and richness, so I say go for it! Combining two dals gives this dish an interesting flavor and texture: yellow split peas are hearty, while the red lentils turn creamy (though you can also use only one dal if you prefer). This is as delicious as it is beautiful, which is why it's one of the most beloved dals in all of South Asia.

DAL

¾ cup toor dal or yellow split peas, rinsed

¼ cup red lentils (masoor dal), rinsed

¼ teaspoon ground turmeric

½ teaspoon fine sea salt

4 cups water, plus more if needed

2 tablespoons chopped cilantro leaves and tender stems, for serving

TARKA BASE

2 tablespoons ghee, store-bought or homemade (page 232), or neutral oil

½ teaspoon cumin seeds

½ medium yellow onion, chopped (½ cup)

1 garlic clove, minced (a generous teaspoon)

1 teaspoon minced ginger

1 large tomato, chopped (about 1½ cups)

¼ teaspoon ground turmeric

½ teaspoon Kashmiri chili powder (see Tip)

½ teaspoon fine sea salt, plus more to taste

TARKA GARNISH

1½ tablespoons ghee, store-bought or homemade (page 232), or neutral oil

½ teaspoon cumin seeds

2 dried red chilies (optional)

¼ teaspoon Kashmiri chili powder (see Tip)

MASALA

1. **Prepare the dals:** In a 3-quart saucepan, place both rinsed dals, the turmeric, salt, and water over high heat. Bring the water to a boil, then reduce the heat to low and cook, partially covered, until the lentils are completely soft, 40 to 50 minutes. Stir occasionally and add more water if the lentils get too dry—they should be very moist but not overly watery. You can test the lentils for doneness by pressing one onto the edge of the pan. They should be completely soft with no visible whiteness at the core; if not, continue cooking, adding ½ cup water if they begin to stick to the bottom of the pan. When they are cooked, mash them with a potato masher to get a loose pea soup–like consistency, with some dal pieces intact and others broken down. Cover and keep the dal warm over very low heat.

2. **Make the tarka base:** Assemble your prepped and measured ingredients by the stove. Heat the ghee in a 10-inch skillet over medium-high heat. Add the cumin seeds, swirl the pan as they sizzle and turn darker, then add the onion and sauté until its edges begin to brown, 3 to 4 minutes. Next, add the garlic and ginger and sauté for a minute, until fragrant. Stir in the tomato, turmeric, Kashmiri chili powder, and salt and sauté for a few minutes, until the tomato breaks down and the mixture is a soft and cohesive mass.

3. Add the onion-tomato tarka base to the cooked dal, along with ½ cup of water, if needed, to get a pourable consistency. (Wipe the skillet clean to use again later.) Stir and simmer for 5 minutes to meld the flavors. Taste and adjust seasoning as needed. (At this point you can cover and set the dal aside until you're ready to serve.

recipe continues

- The mise en place is important for this dish because a lot happens in rapid sequence.
- If you don't have Kashmiri chili powder, use a mixture of 3 parts sweet paprika to 1 part cayenne. Make extra and store it for future use.

SERVING

- Use leftover dal to enrich soups or stews.
- Make a wrap with leftover dal and veggies in a tortilla.
- Enjoy dal with steamed basmati rice and a sautéed vegetable such as Gingered Brussels Sprouts (page 119) or Shredded Beets and Carrots with Sizzled Greens (page 116).

When you are close to serving, rewarm the dal completely, then pour it into a warm serving bowl.)

4. Make the tarka garnish: Assemble your prepped and measured ingredients by the stove. In the same skillet used for the first tarka and wiped clean, heat the ghee. When it shimmers, add the cumin seeds and dried red chilies and give them a few seconds to sizzle in the oil. Add the Kashmiri chili powder, swirl the pan to circulate the spice and briefly cook it, then immediately pour the mixture over the dal. Top with cilantro and serve immediately.

USE AN ELECTRIC PRESSURE COOKER (SUCH AS AN INSTANT POT)

Rinse and drain the dals. Place them in the inner pot with the salt and 3 cups water. Close the vent and cook on high pressure for 10 minutes if using toor dal, 20 if using yellow split peas, and then allow the steam to naturally release. Open the lid and whisk the dal briefly to achieve a creamy consistency. Set on Keep Warm as you move to step 2 and make the tarka base.

GOLDEN TEMPLE DAL

This Amritsari dal is very auspicious to Punjabis, because it is made at gudwaras (Sikh gathering places like the Golden Temple) and offered to all who pass through. My Punjabi friend and product development chef Devika Narula shared her mother's recipe with me. It uses black urad and chana dal, which lend a lovely full flavor. I adapted it to work with black lentils and yellow split peas, which are easier to find. However you choose to make it, it tastes wonderful.

DAL

½ cup black lentils (beluga) or whole black urad dal, rinsed

½ cup yellow split peas or chana dal, rinsed

¼ teaspoon ground turmeric

½ teaspoon fine sea salt

4 to 6 cups water

TARKA

2 tablespoons neutral oil

½ teaspoon cumin seeds

½ medium onion, chopped (½ cup)

1 teaspoon minced garlic

1 teaspoon minced ginger

½ teaspoon minced serrano, or 1 teaspoon minced jalapeño

1 medium tomato, chopped (¾ cup)

MASALA ⎧ 1 teaspoon ground coriander

¼ teaspoon ground turmeric

½ teaspoon Kashmiri chili powder (see Tip)

½ teaspoon fine sea salt

TO FINISH

¼ teaspoon North Indian garam masala, store-bought or homemade (page 222)

2 tablespoons finely chopped cilantro leaves and tender stems

TIP

If you don't have Kashmiri chili powder, use a mixture of 3 parts sweet paprika to 1 part cayenne. Make extra and store it for future use.

SERVING

Enjoy with basmati rice or Tender Chapatis (page 197) and achar (Indian pickle).

1. **Prepare the dal:** In a 3-quart saucepan, combine the rinsed lentils and split peas, turmeric, salt, and 4 cups of the water. Bring to a boil over high heat, then reduce the heat to low. Simmer, partially covered, for 40 to 50 minutes (or 1¼ hours if you're using black urad dal and chana dal), or until the lentils are soft and break easily when pressed against the side of the pan. Check periodically to make sure there's enough water; add more if necessary. The cook time varies, so don't be surprised if your lentils need more time and more water. Remove from the heat, cover the dal, and set it aside.

2. **Make the tarka:** Assemble your prepped and measured ingredients by the stove. In a 10-inch skillet, heat the oil over medium-high heat. When it's shimmering, add the cumin seeds and let them sizzle for a few seconds. Next, add the onion and sauté until the edges are golden brown, 5 to 8 minutes. Add the garlic, ginger, and green chili and stir for a minute, until they lose their raw smell. Next, add the chopped tomato and stir until the tomato breaks down, about 3 minutes. Last, add the coriander, turmeric, Kashmiri chili powder, and salt and sauté for a minute to soften the spices and let the flavors meld. Add a little water if the spices stick to the skillet. Pour the mixture into the dal and stir. Taste and adjust seasoning as needed. (You can prepare the dal ahead of time to this point. When you are ready to serve, make sure the dal is heated through. Adjust with water if it is too thick.)

3. **To finish:** Stir in the garam masala and transfer to a warm serving bowl. Garnish with fresh cilantro and serve.

USE AN ELECTRIC PRESSURE COOKER (SUCH AS AN INSTANT POT)

Rinse and drain the lentils. Place them in the inner pot with turmeric, salt, and 3 cups water. Close the vent and cook on high pressure for 25 minutes (or 35 minutes if using black urad dal and chana dal), then allow the steam to naturally release. Open the lid and whisk the lentils briefly to achieve a creamy consistency. Set on Keep Warm as you move to step 2 and make the tarka.

CREAMY BLACK LENTIL DAL

The original model for this dish, dal makhani, is a rich, dreamy black dal from the Punjab in northwestern India made with black urad dal and kidney beans. I've had great versions in restaurants, but when I looked at recipes to make my own, I was alarmed by the amounts of butter and cream called for (which explains why it's so darn delicious!). I worked out this approach that has much less dairy than the traditional version and uses all black (beluga) lentils, because they're easy to find and fast-cooking. Traditionalists will want to use urad dal (and kidney beans), but either way, it's still extremely yummy—even the vegan version!

DAL

1 cup black lentils (beluga lentils) or whole black urad dal, rinsed

½ teaspoon fine sea salt

3 to 3½ cups water

FLAVOR BASE

2 tablespoons neutral oil

½ large white or yellow onion, diced (1½ cups)

1 medium garlic clove, minced (1 teaspoon)

1 teaspoon minced ginger

2½ tablespoons tomato paste

About 1¾ cups water, plus more if needed

MASALA
1 teaspoon ground cumin

½ teaspoon Kashmiri chili powder (see Tip)

¼ teaspoon North Indian garam masala, store-bought or homemade (page 222)

½ teaspoon fine sea salt

TO FINISH

¼ cup heavy cream or coconut milk

1 tablespoon salted butter (optional)

1 tablespoon chopped cilantro leaves and tender stems

TIPS

• Make this vegan by opting for the coconut milk and omitting the butter.

• A stick blender is handy to have for this one.

• The black lentil, which is black throughout, produces a darker dal, while black urad dal creates a paler result since its interior is creamy white. Mixing them together works nicely, too!

1. **Prepare the dal:** In a 3-quart saucepan, combine the rinsed dal, salt, and 3 cups water (or 3½ cups if using black urad dal) over high heat. Bring it to a boil, then reduce the heat to low, partially cover, and simmer for 35 minutes (or 50 minutes for black urad dal), or until the lentils are cooked through and tender. Remove from the heat, cover, and set aside.

2. **Make the flavor base:** Assemble your prepped and measured ingredients by the stove. In a 10-inch sauté pan, heat the oil over medium-high heat. Add the onions and sauté them, stirring occasionally, until the edges begin to brown, 5 to 8 minutes. Add the garlic and ginger and stir for about a minute, until they become fragrant. Add the tomato paste and ⅓ cup of the water, reduce the heat to medium, and stir for a couple of minutes to blend the flavors. Add the ground cumin, Kashmiri chili powder, garam masala, and salt and sauté until fragrant, about a minute. Remove from the heat.

3. Add the flavor base and 1 cup of the water to the reserved beans and stir over medium heat until heated through. Reduce the heat to low and continue cooking, partially covered, for 15 minutes more to meld the flavors.

4. Remove the dal from the heat and partially puree the mixture using a stick blender or food processor. If it's very thick, add another ½ cup of the water, or more if necessary. Be careful not to overprocess it; the goal is to break down about half of the lentils to create a creamy texture with many visible whole lentils remaining.

• If you don't have Kashmiri chili powder, use a mixture of 3 parts sweet paprika to 1 part cayenne. Make extra and store it for future use.

SERVING

• Serve with Garlic Naan (page 194) and Chicken Tikka Skewers (page 157).
• Spread a generous layer on a plate and top with pan-roasted fish or sliced chicken breast.
• Spoon it on a baked potato with a dollop of Greek yogurt.

Taste and adjust seasonings as needed. (The dal may be prepared ahead of time up to this stage. Be sure to reheat it before serving.)

5. **To finish:** Pour the dal into a warm serving bowl and stir in the cream. As a finishing touch, place the pat of butter on top so it melts into the dal and sprinkle with chopped cilantro. Serve immediately.

USE AN ELECTRIC PRESSURE COOKER (SUCH AS AN INSTANT POT)

Rinse and drain the dal. Place it in the inner pot with salt and 3 cups water (for both lentils and urad dal). Close the vent and cook on high pressure for 15 minutes for black lentils, 20 minutes for urad dal, then allow the pressure to release naturally. Open the lid and whisk the lentils briefly to achieve a creamy consistency. Set on Keep Warm as you move to step 2 and make the flavor base.

COCONUT MOONG DAL

In Kerala, this simple, creamy, homestyle dal is known as parippu. It gets its special flavor from the coconut paste and the curry leaf tarka. My Aunty Kamala made this one regularly, so the aroma of it takes me straight back to her kitchen—especially when I use coconut oil.

DAL

1 cup yellow moong dal, rinsed

¼ teaspoon ground turmeric

½ teaspoon fine sea salt

4 cups water, plus more if needed

COCONUT PASTE

¾ cup dried unsweetened shredded coconut

½ teaspoon cumin seeds

1 serrano or jalapeño, coarsely chopped

1 small shallot, coarsely chopped (⅓ cup)

½ teaspoon fine sea salt

½ to 1 cup water

TARKA

1 tablespoon unrefined coconut oil or neutral oil

½ teaspoon brown or black mustard seeds

10 to 12 fresh curry leaves (1 inch or longer; optional but ideal)

1 dried red chili, or ⅛ teaspoon dried red chili flakes

1 large shallot, thinly sliced crosswise (½ cup)

TIP

If you're using coconut oil, choose unrefined coconut oil, also labeled virgin or extra-virgin.

SERVING

• Serve this over steamed rice with a spoonful of Ghee (page 232).

• Add this to a grain bowl with farro, wilted greens, and roasted squash.

• Add coconut milk to leftover dal and turn it into a soup.

1. **Prepare the dal:** In a 3-quart saucepan, combine the rinsed dal, turmeric, salt, and water over high heat. When the dal comes to a boil, reduce the heat to low, partially cover, and cook for 25 to 30 minutes, or until the dal is soft when pressed with a spoon. Check periodically to make sure it isn't sticking to the bottom of the pan and add more water if it dries out. Cover and set aside.

2. **Make the coconut paste:** While the dal is cooking, combine the coconut, cumin seeds, green chili, chopped shallot, salt, and ½ cup water in a mini food processor or blender. Process to a thick paste, frequently scraping down the sides and adding more water if needed to make it smooth, like a thick pesto.

3. When the dal has finished cooking, pour the coconut paste into it. If the dal is thick, use an extra ½ cup water (or more) to swirl the remaining paste out of the processor and add that, too; stir to combine. Taste and adjust the seasoning as needed. (You can prepare the dal ahead of time to this point and keep it covered for a few hours. When you're ready to serve, turn the heat to medium and warm the dal through, stirring occasionally to prevent sticking.) Transfer it to a warm serving bowl.

4. **Make the tarka:** Assemble your prepped and measured ingredients by the stove. In an 8-inch skillet, heat the coconut oil over medium-high heat. When the oil shimmers, add the mustard seeds and let them pop, occasionally swirling the pan. After they have popped for a few seconds, add the curry leaves and, after they crackle, add the dried red chili and the sliced shallot and sauté for 2 minutes, until the shallot turns brown. Pour the mixture over the dal and serve immediately.

USE AN ELECTRIC PRESSURE COOKER (SUCH AS AN INSTANT POT)

Rinse and drain the dal. Place it in the inner pot with the turmeric, salt, and 3 cups water. Close the vent and cook on high pressure for 5 minutes, then allow it to naturally release. Open the lid and whisk the lentils briefly to achieve a creamy consistency. Set on Keep Warm as you move to step 2 and make the coconut paste.

RED LENTIL DAL WITH SPINACH

MASALA

DAL

1 cup red lentils (masoor dal), rinsed

¼ teaspoon ground turmeric

½ teaspoon fine sea salt

4 cups water, plus more if needed

TARKA

3 tablespoons neutral oil

1½ teaspoons cumin seeds

¼ teaspoon dried red chili flakes

1 large garlic clove, minced (2 teaspoons)

1 teaspoon minced serrano, or 1½ teaspoons minced jalapeño

1 medium tomato, chopped (1 cup)

½ teaspoon turmeric

⅛ teaspoon asafetida (optional)

½ teaspoon fine sea salt

5 ounces baby spinach or regular spinach, tough stems removed and discarded, leaves chopped medium-fine (about 4 cups)

2 teaspoons fresh lemon juice

TIP

Prewashed baby spinach works well in this dish—no trimming required.

SERVING

• Serve with steamed rice and your favorite chili crisp.

• For a quick lunch, spoon this over thick toast and top with yogurt.

I love this dal because it cooks quickly, and the spinach makes it feel extra nourishing. I could eat it over a bowl of steamed rice and feel totally fulfilled. Asafetida is a nice-to-have ingredient here. It's not essential to the dish, but it adds a subtle oniony quality, plus it's meant to make beans more digestible, so use it if you have it!

1. **Prepare the dal:** In a 3-quart saucepan, combine the rinsed lentils, turmeric, salt, and water and bring to a boil over high heat. Reduce the heat to low, partially cover, and cook until the lentils are soft, about 25 minutes. (Partially covering the lentils ensures that the water doesn't evaporate or boil over as they cook.) Stir them periodically to make sure they aren't sticking to the bottom, and add more water if they dry out. When soft, remove from the heat and set aside.

2. **Make the tarka:** After the dal has cooked, assemble your prepped and measured ingredients by the stove. Heat the oil in a deep 11- to 12-inch skillet over medium-high heat. When the oil shimmers, add the cumin seeds and red chili flakes and fry for a few seconds until fragrant. Add the garlic, green chili, and tomato and stir constantly for a few minutes, until the tomato turns soft. Add the turmeric, asafetida, and salt and stir well. Last, add half of the spinach and stir for 2 minutes until it wilts, then add the remaining spinach and cook for a few more minutes, until wilted but still bright green. Pour the entire mixture into the dal and stir. Taste and adjust seasoning as needed. (The dal can be prepared ahead of time to this point, covered, and set aside. When you're ready to serve, warm the dal through completely.)

3. To finish, stir in the lemon juice and serve.

USE AN ELECTRIC PRESSURE COOKER (SUCH AS AN INSTANT POT)

Rinse and drain the lentils. Place them in the inner pot with the turmeric, salt, and 3 cups water. Close the vent and cook on high pressure for 5 minutes, then allow the steam to naturally release. Open the lid and whisk the lentils briefly to achieve a creamy consistency. Set on Keep Warm as you move to step 2 and make the tarka.

TEA-BRAISED PUNJABI CHICKPEAS

Infusing chickpeas with tea is a trick I learned from my friend Devika Narula. It's a Punjabi tradition that adds deeper color to beans and the finished dish. This is a great curry regardless of whether you like tea!

TEA

1 English breakfast tea bag or another strong, unflavored black tea (see Tip)

1½ cups water

CHICKPEAS

3 tablespoons neutral oil

½ teaspoon cumin seeds

1 large yellow onion, finely chopped (about 2½ cups)

2 medium garlic cloves, minced (2 teaspoons)

2 teaspoons minced ginger

1 serrano or jalapeño, split in half lengthwise

2 medium tomatoes, pureed (about 1½ cups)

1 teaspoon ground coriander

1 teaspoon ground cumin

¼ teaspoon ground turmeric

¾ teaspoon Kashmiri chili powder (see Tip)

½ teaspoon North Indian garam masala, store-bought or homemade (page 222)

1 teaspoon fine sea salt

2 (15-ounce) cans chickpeas, drained and rinsed

MASALA

TO FINISH

1 teaspoon fresh lemon juice

3 tablespoons chopped cilantro leaves and tender stems

1. **Make the tea:** In a small saucepan over high heat, bring the water to a boil. Turn off the heat, add the tea bag, and steep for 5 minutes. Remove the bag and set the tea aside.

2. **Prepare the chickpeas:** Assemble all your prepped and measured ingredients by the stove. In a wide, deep skillet, heat the oil over medium-high. When the oil shimmers, add the cumin seeds and sizzle for a few seconds. Add the onion and stir frequently until the edges are lightly browned, 5 to 8 minutes. Add the garlic, ginger, and green chili and sauté until fragrant, about 1 minute. Stir in the tomato puree, reduce the heat to medium, and stir occasionally until most of the liquid disappears and the mixture starts to come together, about 5 minutes. Add the coriander, cumin, turmeric, Kashmiri chili powder, garam masala, and salt and stir constantly for a minute until the spices lose their raw smell (add a little water if the spices stick to the skillet).

3. Add the chickpeas and tea to the skillet, increase the heat to medium-high, and bring the mixture to a boil. Reduce the heat to low, cover, and simmer for 10 to 15 minutes, until the chickpeas are nice and soft. Add more water if the chickpeas dry out. At this point, you can mash up some of the chickpeas with the back of a spoon or with a potato masher to help thicken the sauce. Remove the curry from the heat. (If you are making this ahead, you can cover and set it aside at this point. Just prior to serving, heat it through completely. You may need to add ¼ to ½ cup water, since it thickens as it sits.)

4. **To finish:** Stir in the lemon juice and cilantro, taste for seasoning, and serve.

TIPS

• Use a strong black tea like PG Tips.

• If you don't have Kashmiri chili powder, use a mixture of 3 parts sweet paprika to 1 part cayenne.

SERVING

• Scoop this up with Tender Chapatis (page 197).

• Stuff this into pita bread and top with Pickled Red Onion (page 230).

• Enjoy the chickpeas over steamed quinoa with yogurt.

COMFORTING CHICKPEAS AND POTATOES

Here is my idea of a cozy bowl of goodness, and it was inspired by a dish from an excellent local Indian restaurant, Cinnamon. This curry doesn't have a specific regional provenance, as Indians all over the subcontinent find delicious ways to combine chickpeas and potatoes. It brings North and South Indian flavors together into a tasty pan-Indian curry.

1. **Make the flavor base:** In a deep 10-inch sauté pan, heat the oil over medium-high heat until shimmering. Add the onion and sauté, stirring frequently until the edges are nicely browned, 5 to 8 minutes. Add the garlic, ginger, and green chili and sauté until fragrant, about 1 minute. Add the tomato and continue stirring until the tomato begins to break down, 3 to 4 minutes. Reduce the heat to medium and add the curry powder, cumin, turmeric, and salt and stir until the spices have mellowed, about 1 minute.

2. **Prepare the chickpeas and potatoes:** Add the chickpeas, potatoes, and water to the pan and stir to combine the ingredients and scrape up any spices stuck to the bottom. Reduce the heat to low, cover, and cook until the potatoes are tender when pierced with a sharp knife, about 20 minutes. Taste and adjust the seasoning as needed. (You can prepare this dish ahead up to this point and rewarm it before serving.)

3. **To finish:** Right before serving, bring the mixture to a simmer over medium heat. Stir in the coconut milk, lemon juice, and cilantro and cook until it is heated through. Stir in the garam masala and transfer to a warm serving bowl. Garnish with extra cilantro if you like. Serve immediately.

FLAVOR BASE

2 tablespoons neutral oil

2 medium yellow onions, chopped into ½-inch dice (2 cups)

1 large garlic clove, minced (2 teaspoons)

2 teaspoons minced ginger

1 teaspoon minced green serrano, jalapeño, or Thai bird chili

1 large tomato, chopped (1½ cups)

3 teaspoons Madras curry powder, store-bought or homemade (page 225)

½ teaspoon ground cumin

¼ teaspoon ground turmeric

1¼ teaspoons fine sea salt

MASALA

CHICKPEAS AND POTATOES

2 (15-ounce) cans chickpeas, drained and rinsed

2 Yukon Gold or other waxy potatoes, peeled and cut into 1-inch cubes (2 cups)

1½ cups water

TO FINISH

1 cup full-fat canned coconut milk

2 teaspoons fresh lemon juice

2 tablespoons chopped cilantro leaves and tender stems, plus extra (optional) for garnish

½ teaspoon North Indian garam masala, store-bought or homemade (page 222)

TIP

Because this dish is pulled together in minutes, prep the ingredients the night before for an easy weeknight main course.

SERVING

• This is perfect with a bowl of brown rice and a kale salad.

• Make it into wraps with warm flour tortillas and yogurt.

MEAT AND SEAFOOD

This chapter features my favorite dishes that rarely get any spotlight in North America. I'm specifically referring to recipes that reflect my South Indian Keralan roots and the foods I've been eating since childhood. Kerala is an anomaly in India because of its unique combination of tropical climate and religious diversity, which gives it a coconut-rich, nonvegetarian cuisine all its own. Dive in and discover Peppery Beef Curry (page 166), Red Chili Shrimp (page 169), and Fish Molee with Fresh Tomato and Coconut (page 172). If you haven't tasted them before, these dishes will offer a whole new set of Indian flavors.

You'll find some familiar friends in this chapter as well. Dishes like Chicken Tikka Skewers (the grilled version, not chicken tikka masala), page 157, my take on tandoori chicken, and Turkey Keema with Sweet Potatoes (page 158) will bring you comfort as they simultaneously reflect a twist in techniques or ingredients. I show you how to char lemon and onion to accompany a whole roasted tandoori chicken, and add lime zest to a chicken tikka marinade. Leg of lamb turns succulent on the grill after marinating in yogurt and herbs. Whether you want to grill with an Indian flair, have a lush tropical fish dish, or enjoy a warm and cozy curry, I've got your meat and fish needs covered.

CHICKEN CHETTINAD WITH BLACK PEPPER COCONUT MASALA

1½ pounds boneless, skinless chicken thighs

COCONUT PASTE

½ cup dried unsweetened shredded coconut

½ cup water

SAUCE

1 teaspoon black peppercorns

½ teaspoon fennel seeds

3 tablespoons neutral oil

1 large onion, cut into ¼-inch dice (about 2½ cups)

1 large garlic clove, minced (2 teaspoons)

2 teaspoons minced ginger

10 to 12 fresh curry leaves (1 inch or longer; optional)

2 medium tomatoes, cut into ½-inch dice (1½ cups)

1 star anise

5 teaspoons Madras curry powder, store-bought or homemade (page 225)

½ teaspoon Kerala Garam Masala (page 224; optional)

¼ teaspoon cayenne

¼ teaspoon ground turmeric

1¼ teaspoons fine sea salt

¼ cup water

2 tablespoons chopped cilantro leaves and tender stems, for garnish

MASALA

This fabulous chicken curry has a rich, deep flavor and an interesting backstory. It comes from the Chettiars, a prosperous community of bankers from Tamil Nadu who conducted business all over South Asia in the eighteenth century and were in turn influenced by the nonvegetarian foods of Kerala, Ceylon, and Burma. Other hallmarks of Chettiar cooking are complex sauces made with black pepper, cinnamon, clove, fennel, and red chili. A feature of this dish is toasted coconut, which is ground into a paste and used to thicken the sauce and give it wonderful, toasty flavor.

1. Trim the chicken thighs and cut them into 1½-inch chunks. Set aside.

2. **Make the coconut paste:** In an 8-inch skillet, stir the coconut continuously over medium-low heat until it turns medium brown and fragrant, about 5 minutes. Don't rush this step, and also make sure you keep an eye on the pan—it's important to evenly brown the coconut for the best flavor, but it can also easily burn. Tip it onto a plate and cool for 5 minutes.

3. Place the toasted coconut in a mini food processor or blender with ¼ cup of the water and grind to a paste, scraping down the sides as needed to process fully. Pour the mixture into a small bowl. Pour the remaining ¼ cup water into the processor, pulse to swish out the residual coconut, and stir the water into the bowl of coconut paste. Set aside.

4. **Prepare the sauce:** Using a mortar and pestle, crush the black peppercorns and fennel to a coarse powder, or place them in an electric spice grinder and give them six or seven quick pulses (alternatively, you can chop them with a chef's knife). Set aside.

recipe continues

- Watch the coconut like a hawk while it toasts and stir it constantly, shaking the pan simultaneously because it can easily burn.
- In this recipe, the curry leaves are not fried in a tempering step as we usually do. Instead their flavor is coaxed out through gentle sautéing.

SERVING

- Serve this over steamed rice with Easy Peas Poriyal (page 113).
- Scoop it up with Tender Chapatis (page 197) or parathas (sold at Indian grocery stores).
- Skip the carbs and serve it with riced cauliflower and sautéed greens.

5. Place the oil in a deep 11- to 12-inch skillet over medium-high heat. When the oil shimmers, add the onion and sauté until well browned around the edges, about 8 minutes. Add the garlic, ginger, and curry leaves and stir until fragrant, about 1 minute. Reduce the heat to medium and add the tomato, the star anise, and the crushed black pepper and fennel and continue to sauté until the tomato breaks down and starts to form a paste, 4 to 6 minutes. Add the curry powder, garam masala, cayenne, turmeric, salt, and water and stir until the spices lose their raw smell, about 1 minute.

6. Add the chicken and continue stirring over medium heat until it loses its pink color, about 5 minutes. Add the toasted coconut paste, increase the heat to medium-high, and bring the mixture to a boil. When it bubbles, reduce the heat to low and simmer, partially covered, until the chicken is cooked through and the ingredients are well blended, about 20 minutes, stirring occasionally and checking the liquid level. The sauce should be juicy but not runny, so remove the lid if necessary to let any excess water cook off.

7. Transfer the curry to a warmed, wide serving bowl, garnish with the chopped cilantro, and serve.

TANDOORI ROASTED CHICKEN WITH CHARRED LEMON AND ONION

1 recipe Favorite Tandoori Marinade (page 227)

1 (3½- to 4½-pound) whole chicken, giblets removed

Kosher salt and freshly ground black pepper

1 large red or sweet onion

1 large lemon

1 tablespoon neutral oil

TIP

If you don't have a roasting rack and pan combo, place the chicken on a large parchment-lined baking sheet instead, and don't add any water to the pan.

SERVING

• Serve with Herby Roasted Potatoes (page 98). Just raise the oven temp after the bird is cooked to finish the potatoes.

• Have with Root Vegetable Mash with Shallot Tarka (page 128) and a kale salad.

I've always enjoyed the way Indian restaurants present tandoori chicken on a smoking hot griddle, with sizzling onions and lemon wedges perfuming the room—my inspiration for the charred lemon and onion here. Mine lacks the intense redness of the restaurant version because I don't use any food coloring, but it has become a favorite in my household because it is so crisp and flavorful and a nice change from basic roasted chicken. And by the way, this marinade can easily be used on boneless chicken breasts, lamb steaks, shrimp, or paneer. Just marinate them as long as possible and grill, roast, or sear, depending on your preference.

1. **Prepare the chicken:** Smear 2 tablespoons of the marinade in the cavity of the chicken, then carefully spread as much marinade as possible under the skin in the following way: Separate the skin from the meat by sliding a finger under the skin and gently sweeping it back and forth over the breast meat, the legs, and the thighs. Be gentle and do your best not to poke a hole in the skin. Then, gently massage the mixture evenly over the meat, underneath the skin. With the small amount of marinade remaining, spread it all over the outside of the bird. Cover and marinate at room temperature for one to two hours. (At this point, you can refrigerate the chicken overnight. Allow the chicken to sit at room temperature for an hour before roasting.)

2. Preheat the oven to 400°F.

3. Place the chicken on a rack set in a roasting pan. Sprinkle lightly with salt and pepper. Pour a little water into the roasting pan, to a depth of about ¼ inch, to prevent the drippings from burning. Place the chicken in the center of the oven and roast until it is golden and the juices run clear when the leg/thigh joint is pierced with a knife, 1 to 1¼ hours, depending on the size of your bird. If the chicken begins to get too brown before it's finished cooking, tent it with foil. Check the chicken from time to time to be sure there is enough liquid in the roasting pan.

recipe continues

4. **Char the onion and lemon:** While the chicken is roasting, peel the onion and cut it crosswise into ½-inch slices, keeping the rings intact. Heat a grill pan or large cast-iron skillet over medium-high heat. Brush each onion slice with some of the oil and place it in the pan. It's time to turn on your vent! Cut the lemon into quarters, removing any noticeable seeds. Brush the quarters with oil and set them in the pan with the onions if there is room; otherwise grill them after the onion is done. Cook the onion and lemon until they have black char marks, about 5 minutes. Carefully flip them to char the other side, another 5 minutes. Transfer everything to a serving platter.

5. When the chicken is roasted, remove it from the oven, transfer it to a cutting board, and let it rest for about 10 minutes. Meanwhile, place the roasting pan over medium heat, scrape up any caramelized bits on the bottom of the pan with a spoon or whisk, and cook until thickened, 3 to 5 minutes. Strain the juices into a small serving bowl or pitcher.

6. Place the serving platter with the onion and lemon in the oven to warm in its residual heat.

7. Carve the chicken and place the pieces on the warmed platter with the onion and lemon pieces. Using tongs, pick up and squeeze a grilled lemon quarter over the chicken pieces. Serve immediately, with the cooking juices on the side.

CHICKEN TIKKA SKEWERS

The word *tikka* means "pieces," as in seared boneless chicken pieces—a dish brought to India by the Mughals from Central Asia. Traditionally, the meat was marinated in yogurt with garlic, ginger, and other spices, threaded on long skewers, and quickly roasted in clay ovens, or tandoors. My version takes the flavor further with the added zippiness of lime zest! These morsels are succulent on their own, but as British Indian restaurants discovered, they are also delicious simmered in a creamy tomato sauce—the dish everyone recognizes as chicken tikka masala.

MARINADE

¼ cup neutral oil

1 medium garlic clove, minced (1 teaspoon)

1 teaspoon finely grated ginger

1 tablespoon finely grated lime zest

¼ cup plain whole milk Greek-style yogurt

MASALA

4 teaspoons ground coriander

2 teaspoons ground cumin

¼ teaspoon ground turmeric

¼ teaspoon cayenne

½ teaspoon North Indian garam masala, store-bought or homemade (page 222)

1¼ teaspoons fine sea salt

1½ pounds chicken tenders or boneless, skinless breasts or thighs, patted dry, trimmed, and cut lengthwise into 1½ × 3-inch strips

GARNISHES

A few sprigs of cilantro

Lime wedges (optional)

TIPS

• This amount of marinade can easily stretch for 2 pounds of chicken to feed 6 people.

• Drizzle the cooked skewers with warm melted ghee, store-bought or homemade (page 232), for a decadent flourish.

SERVING

• Fold into lettuce wraps with Pickled Red Onion (page 230), Greek yogurt, and fresh herbs.

• Chop any leftovers for a chicken salad with mayo and scallions.

1. If you're using bamboo skewers rather than metal, place eight of them in a 9 × 13-inch baking pan, cover with water, and soak for at least 30 minutes.

2. **Marinate the chicken:** Mix all the marinade ingredients together in a large bowl. Add the chicken, toss together until coated, and set aside to marinate for 1 hour at room temperature, or up to overnight in the refrigerator. (Remove from the refrigerator at least 30 minutes prior to cooking).

3. Preheat the broiler to high. Set the rack 3 inches from the heat source.

4. Thread the chicken pieces onto the soaked skewers in a wavy pattern, piercing each piece multiple times to secure it on the stick. Do not press the pieces closely together but allow space between them so they cook thoroughly. Place the skewers on a broiling pan and broil until they are golden and opaque on one side, about 4 minutes. Turn and broil the other side until golden, 4 to 5 minutes. The chicken should be thoroughly cooked but not dry; to test, cut into one of the chicken pieces. If the chicken is still slightly pink, continue cooking another minute or two. Remove from the oven when done and set aside. (If using a grill, when the grill is hot, cook the skewers for about 4 minutes per side.)

5. Serve the chicken either on or off the skewers, arranged on a platter and scattered with cilantro sprigs and lime wedges.

TURKEY KEEMA WITH SWEET POTATOES

Keema, a North Indian ground meat curry, is one of the most comforting dishes in India. My dad used to make it the classic way, with lamb and potatoes, but I like switching it up by using turkey and sweet potatoes. The sweetness is a nice contrast with the gentle spice of the dish. No matter the meat you use, or if you choose a plant-based meat replacement, I predict you'll love this keema because it's a brilliant solution for what to do with a pound of ground anything.

MASALA

6 teaspoons ground coriander

1 teaspoon ground cumin

¼ teaspoon cayenne

¼ teaspoon freshly ground black pepper

¼ teaspoon ground turmeric

⅛ teaspoon ground cinnamon

⅛ teaspoon ground clove

3 tablespoons neutral oil

2 medium yellow onions, chopped medium (2 cups)

1 large garlic clove, minced (2 teaspoons)

2 teaspoons minced ginger

1 teaspoon minced serrano, or 2 teaspoons minced jalapeño

1 pound ground turkey

1 teaspoon fine sea salt

1 large sweet potato, peeled and cut into ¼-inch cubes (2 cups)

1 medium tomato, chopped (1 cup)

1 cup water

1 cup frozen peas

TO FINISH

1 teaspoon fresh lemon juice

2 tablespoons chopped cilantro leaves and tender stems

SERVING

• Keema is perfect with steamed basmati rice and Minty Cucumber Raita (page 86).

• This also makes a great filling for stuffed peppers.

• Use this as a base for shepherd's pie.

1. In a small bowl, combine the ground spices and set aside. Heat the oil in a large 11- to 12-inch sauté pan (with a lid) over medium-high heat. When it is shimmering, add the onion and cook, stirring, until the edges are golden, about 8 minutes. Stir in the garlic, ginger, and green chili and cook until they become fragrant, about 1 minute. Add the ground meat and cook, breaking it up into small pieces with a spatula, until it browns a bit at the edges, 5 to 7 minutes.

2. Stir in the ground spices and salt and sauté over medium heat until the spices lose their raw smell, 1 to 2 minutes. Add the sweet potato, tomato, and water and stir to blend well. Bring the mixture to a boil, then reduce the heat to low so the liquid is just simmering. Cover and cook until the potato and tomato are soft and the meat is cooked through, about 25 minutes. Stir the mixture occasionally to make sure it is cooking evenly.

3. Add the peas and cook another 2 to 3 minutes. If it seems watery at this point, remove the cover to evaporate some of the liquid until the sauce is thick but still moist.

4. **To finish:** Stir in the lemon juice and cilantro and transfer to a warm bowl. Serve immediately.

RICH KERALA EGG ROAST

In Kerala, "egg roast" is an iconic dish, and anyone who has tried it knows it's a disarmingly delicious curry of boiled eggs in a thick caramelized onion sauce. In Keralan cooking, "roasts" have nothing to do with ovens; rather, they involve marinating meat or seafood, then sautéing it with just enough other ingredients to create a sticky sauce that clings to the surface.

8 large eggs

SPICE PASTE

1 teaspoon fennel seeds

3 teaspoons ground coriander

2 teaspoons ground cumin

1½ teaspoons Madras curry powder, store-bought or homemade (page 225)

⅓ cup water

TARKA

3 tablespoons neutral oil

1 teaspoon brown or black mustard seeds

12 to 15 fresh curry leaves (1 inch or longer; optional)

1 whole dried red chili, or ⅛ teaspoon dried red chili flakes

1 large onion, sliced (about 2½ cups)

1 medium tomato, chopped (1 cup)

1 teaspoon fine sea salt, plus more to taste

TO FINISH

½ cup full-fat canned coconut milk

½ cup water, plus more if needed

TIP

You can boil the eggs the night before you make the dish.

SERVING

• Spoon this over steamed rice with a side of Roasted Asparagus with Tamarind and Crispy Shallots (page 102).

• Serve with flaky parathas, available at Indian grocery stores.

MASALA

1. Place a medium pot of water over high heat and bring the water to a boil. Carefully add the eggs using a slotted spoon, reduce the heat to medium-low so the water is bubbling gently, and boil the eggs for 8 minutes for slightly soft yolks or 11 minutes for firmer yolks. Transfer the eggs to a bowl of ice water. When the eggs are cool, remove the shells. Halve each egg lengthwise and set aside.

2. **Prepare the spice paste:** Crush the fennel seeds to a coarse powder in a mortar and pestle or with six or seven quick pulses in an electric spice grinder (alternatively, chop them with a chef's knife). Place the crushed fennel in a small bowl. Add the coriander, cumin, curry powder, and water to make a watery paste (this prevents the spices from scorching in the pan).

3. **Make the tarka:** Assemble your prepped and measured ingredients by the stove. In a wide nonstick skillet, heat the oil over medium-high heat. When the oil is shimmering, add the mustard seeds and allow them to pop, occasionally swirling the pan. After they have popped for a few seconds, toss in the curry leaves and let them crackle. Next, add the dried red chili, stir for a few seconds, then add the onion and cook, stirring occasionally, until it is deep brown at the edges, 8 to 10 minutes. Reduce the heat to medium and add the tomato and salt, stirring occasionally, until the tomato is soft and breaks down, 2 to 3 minutes. Add the spice paste and stir frequently until the spices lose their raw smell, 1 to 2 minutes. Add a little more water, if necessary, to keep the spices from sticking to the bottom of the pan.

4. **To finish:** Stir in the coconut milk and water, and mix until thoroughly combined. Simmer for 1 minute. Add the halved eggs, spooning the sauce over them and shaking the pan gently so the yolks and the whites stay together while the eggs heat through. Remove from the heat and taste for salt. Carefully transfer to a warmed, shallow bowl and serve immediately.

CLASSIC PORK VINDALOO

This Portuguese-Goan favorite is famously full of heat and tang plus umami richness so that everything is in balance and the fire is never out of control. The key is long, slow braising to allow plenty of time to tenderize the meat and intensify the flavors. I also suggest keeping the sides simple and light so that the vindaloo can shine in the spotlight.

2½ to 3 pounds boneless pork shoulder or butt

MARINADE

MASALA

8 teaspoons ground coriander

2 teaspoons ground cumin

½ teaspoon cayenne

½ teaspoon freshly ground black pepper

¼ teaspoon ground turmeric

⅛ teaspoon ground cinnamon

⅛ teaspoon ground cloves

⅓ cup white vinegar

SAUCE

½ teaspoon brown or black mustard seeds

1 teaspoon tamarind paste or concentrate

2 tablespoons warm water

4 tablespoons neutral oil

1 large yellow onion, sliced thin (about 2½ cups)

2 teaspoons minced garlic

2 teaspoons minced ginger

2 to 3 green chilies, split lengthwise, with tops intact

1 large tomato, chopped (1½ cups)

1 teaspoon fine sea salt

TO FINISH

½ cup full-fat canned coconut milk

¼ cup coarsely chopped cilantro leaves and tender stems

SERVING

• Serve with Basmati with Shallots and Cumin (page 182) and Minty Cucumber Raita (page 86)

• Have this with Tender Chapatis (page 197) or tortillas and a green salad.

1. Trim the fat off the pork and cut it into 1½-inch chunks.

2. **Marinate the pork:** In a large nonreactive bowl, combine all the ingredients. Add the pork, mixing to coat it well, cover, and marinate in the refrigerator for at least 4 hours and as long as 24 hours.

3. **Prepare the sauce:** Partially crush the mustard seeds in a mortar and pestle or electric spice grinder until they appear half brown, half yellow; set aside. In a small bowl, dilute the tamarind in the warm water; set aside.

4. Heat 1 tablespoon of the oil in a Dutch oven or a deep 11- to 12-inch skillet over medium-high heat. When the oil shimmers, add all the pork pieces, reserving the marinade liquid, and stir every few minutes for 5 to 8 minutes, until lightly colored on all sides. Remove the pork to a plate.

5. In the same pan, heat the remaining 3 tablespoons oil over medium-high heat and sauté the onion until deep golden, 7 to 10 minutes. Add the garlic, ginger, and the green chili and sauté for 1 minute, until fragrant. Add the crushed mustard seeds, tomato, salt, and diluted tamarind and continue to sauté until the tomato has softened, 2 to 3 minutes. Return the pork along with the reserved marinade liquid to the pot and stir well. It may look like it needs water, but the meat will release liquid as it cooks. When the sauce comes to a boil, reduce the heat to low. Cover and simmer gently for 1 hour, then check to see if the meat is fully cooked. Don't be surprised if it takes another 30 minutes, or possibly even longer, to become fork-tender. (The dish can be prepared ahead of time up to this point, if you like. Reheat before proceeding.)

6. **To finish:** When the pork is completely tender, increase the heat to medium. Stir in the coconut milk and gently simmer for 15 minutes, until the sauce is thick and dark. If it looks dry add a little water. Remove it from the heat and transfer to a warmed serving bowl. Garnish with the chopped cilantro and serve.

GRILLED LEG OF LAMB WITH YOGURT-HERB MARINADE

1 (5- to 7-pound) leg of lamb, boned so it lies flat

MARINADE

1 tablespoon cumin seeds

½ bunch cilantro leaves and tender stems, coarsely chopped (about 1 cup)

Leaves from a bunch of mint (about 1 cup gently packed)

3 medium garlic cloves

2 teaspoons chopped ginger

Grated zest of ½ lemon

1 cup plain whole milk Greek-style yogurt

1 teaspoon fine sea salt

Freshly ground black pepper

Cilantro and mint sprigs, for garnish

TIP

The lamb can also be roasted in the oven: cook it in a roasting pan (no need to sear) at 450°F for 25 to 35 minutes, or until a meat thermometer reads 120°F for rare or 130°F for medium.

SERVING

• Serve with Tamil Lemon Rice (page 183) or Herby Roasted Potatoes (page 98) and a Greek salad on the side.

• Enjoy with orzo, green beans, and Roasted Tomato Tarka with Yogurt (page 64).

Lamb, yogurt, herbs, and garlic have a natural affinity for each other in a way that transcends borders, so combining them here felt natural and coherent. While this dish is reminiscent of Greek and Middle Eastern lamb preparations, the toasted cumin adds a distinctly Indian inflection.

1. Remove and discard the fat cap from the lamb and pat the meat dry with paper towels. Set it aside in a nonreactive bowl.

2. **Prepare the marinade:** In a small skillet, toast the cumin seeds over medium heat, stirring until darker brown and fragrant (they will smoke slightly), about 2 minutes. Turn them out onto a plate to cool, then grind them to a fine powder with a mortar and pestle or electric spice grinder. Tip the cumin into the bowl of a food processor and add the cilantro, mint, garlic, ginger, lemon zest, yogurt, salt, and many grinds of pepper and puree until mostly smooth. Spread the marinade over the lamb, coating it completely, then cover and marinate in the refrigerator for 1 to 3 hours. Allow the lamb to sit at room temperature for 1 hour before grilling.

3. Preheat the grill to medium-high. When it is hot, spread the lamb on the grates in a single layer and cook until seared, 5 minutes. Flip it and cook the other side for about 5 minutes, or until seared to your taste. Lower the cover, reduce the heat to medium-low, and continue cooking for 20 minutes. Flip the lamb and cook another 20 minutes. Check the temperature at thickest part: it should read 120°F for rare or 130°F for medium. There should be a hint of pink when you cut into it; cook further if needed. Transfer the lamb to a cutting board that will catch the juices and let it rest for 10 minutes. Slice and serve, garnished with sprigs of cilantro and mint and drizzled with the juices.

PEPPERY BEEF CURRY

Many assume that all Indians eschew beef, but the truth is more complicated. A large number of Hindus don't eat beef; however, my family comes from Kerala, a state with a well-established Christian population, known for their delicious food, including beef curries like this one. This recipe uses black pepper, fennel, coconut, and curry leaves to complement and amplify the flavor of the beef. I don't eat beef often, but I make an exception for this dish.

TARKA

1 tablespoon black peppercorns

½ teaspoon fennel seeds

3 tablespoons neutral oil

½ teaspoon brown or black mustard seeds

15 to 20 fresh curry leaves (1 inch or longer; optional)

1 large yellow onion, thinly sliced (about 2½ cups)

1 large shallot, thinly sliced crosswise (½ cup)

1 large garlic clove, minced (2 teaspoons)

1 tablespoon minced ginger

2 whole serranos, Thai bird chilies, or small jalapeños, split lengthwise, with tops intact

1 medium tomato, chopped (1 cup)

4½ teaspoons ground coriander

½ teaspoon ground turmeric

¼ teaspoon cayenne

1½ teaspoons Kerala Garam Masala (page 224)

1¼ teaspoons fine sea salt

1½ pounds beef, ideally tenderloin or sirloin, trimmed and cut into 1-inch cubes

½ cup water

TO FINISH

¼ cup full-fat canned coconut milk

8 to 10 whole basil or cilantro leaves (optional)

SERVING

Serve with Root Vegetable Mash with Shallot Tarka (page 128) or polenta and a salad.

MASALA

1. **Make the tarka:** Crush the peppercorns and fennel seeds into a coarse powder in a mortar and pestle or give them six or seven quick pulses in an electric spice grinder (alternatively, chop them with a chef's knife). Set aside. Next, assemble the remaining prepped and measured ingredients for the tarka by the stove.

2. In an 11- to 12-inch sauté pan or Dutch oven, heat the oil over medium-high heat until it shimmers. Add the mustard seeds and allow them to pop, occasionally swirling the pan. After they have popped for a few seconds, add the fresh curry leaves, and after they have crackled for a few seconds, add the onion and shallot and sauté until the onion begins to brown, 6 to 8 minutes. Add the garlic, ginger, and green chilies and sauté until fragrant, about 1 minute. Add the tomato and reduce the heat to medium. Stir the mixture frequently until the tomato begins to break down, about 3 minutes. Add the reserved crushed black pepper and fennel, the coriander, turmeric, cayenne, garam masala, and salt and stir constantly until the spices lose their raw smell, 30 to 60 seconds. If the spices stick to the pan, add a drizzle of water to loosen them.

3. Add the beef cubes and cook, stirring often, until the meat loses its pink color on the surface, about 4 minutes. Add the water, stir, and scrape any spices off the bottom of the pan. Reduce the heat to low and cook, partially covered and stirring occasionally, until the meat is cooked through and the sauce is glistening, 8 to 10 minutes. (This curry will improve from sitting, so you can make it up to this point several hours ahead or even the night before.)

4. **To finish:** Stir in the coconut milk and increase the heat to medium. Simmer for 1 minute and remove from the heat. Serve immediately garnished with fresh herbs.

RED CHILI SHRIMP

This dish is called "prawn roast" because in Kerala, where it's from, the method of dry-frying meat or seafood in a hot pan is referred to as "roasting." The preparation is very traditional, beginning with marinating the shrimp in spices, then making a small amount of thick sauce and folding in the shrimp. Bright red Kashmiri chili powder adds great color without overpowering heat, so I like using it for this dish. I also add a bit of tomato paste to boost the red color even more and to help the sauce cling to the shrimp. It's an easy dish with big flavor.

SHRIMP AND MARINADE

1 pound large shrimp, peeled and deveined

¼ teaspoon Kashmiri chili powder (see Tip)

¼ teaspoon freshly ground black pepper

¼ teaspoon ground turmeric

½ teaspoon fine sea salt

SAUCE

¼ teaspoon fennel seeds

2 tablespoons unrefined coconut oil

½ large yellow onion, diced (1½ cups)

1 large garlic clove, minced (2 teaspoons)

1 teaspoon finely minced ginger

1 teaspoon minced serrano, or 2 teaspoons minced jalapeño

1 tablespoon tomato paste

2 teaspoons ground coriander

1 teaspoon Kashmiri chili powder (see Tip)

½ teaspoon Kerala Garam Masala (page 224)

¼ cup water

½ teaspoon fine sea salt

TARKA

1 tablespoon unrefined coconut oil

10 to 12 fresh curry leaves (1 inch or longer; optional but ideal)

TIP

If you don't have Kashmiri chili powder, use a mixture of 3 parts sweet paprika to 1 part cayenne.

SERVING

Serve the shrimp alongside linguine tossed with sautéed garlic.

1. **Marinate the shrimp:** Pat the shrimp dry with paper towels and place them in a medium bowl. If you prefer the tails removed, take them off. In a small bowl, combine the Kashmiri chili powder, pepper, turmeric, and salt. Add the spice mixture to the shrimp and toss well to combine. Set aside to marinate as you prep the sauce ingredients.

2. **Make the sauce:** Crush the fennel seeds to a coarse powder in a mortar and pestle, or place them in an electric spice grinder and give them six or seven quick pulses (alternatively, you can chop them with a chef's knife). Set aside. Assemble all the prepped and measured sauce ingredients by the stove.

3. Heat the coconut oil in an 11- to 12-inch sauté pan or wok over medium heat. Add the onion and sauté until it begins to brown around the edges. Add the garlic, ginger, and green chili and sauté, stirring, for a minute, until fragrant. Add the reserved crushed fennel, the tomato paste, coriander, Kashmiri chili powder, garam masala, and water and sauté, stirring, until well blended and fragrant.

4. Increase the heat to medium-high and add the shrimp and all the marinade, stirring constantly until the shrimp is gently curled and pink, about 5 minutes. This is a dryish curry, but if it's too dry and sticking to the pan, add water by the tablespoon until you get a thick, sticky sauce that mostly clings to the shrimp. Remove from the heat.

5. **Make the tarka:** In an 8-inch skillet, melt the coconut oil over medium-high heat until it shimmers. Add the curry leaves, and fry for a few seconds until they crackle. Pour over the shrimp and serve immediately.

Fish Molee with
Fresh Tomato
and Coconut

FISH MOLEE WITH FRESH TOMATO AND COCONUT

1¼ pounds skin-on halibut, cod, or haddock fillets or a similarly firm white fish (see Tip)

TARKA

2 tablespoons neutral oil

2 teaspoons minced ginger

12 to 15 fresh curry leaves (1 inch or longer; optional but ideal)

½ large yellow onion, finely chopped (1½ cups)

2 garlic cloves, minced (3 teaspoons)

1 serrano or jalapeño, split lengthwise with top intact

½ teaspoon ground turmeric

¼ teaspoon Kashmiri chili powder (see Tip)

1 teaspoon fine sea salt, plus more to taste

TO FINISH

2 plum tomatoes, sliced crosswise into thin rounds

¾ cup full-fat canned coconut milk

¾ cup water

1 teaspoon white vinegar

1 teaspoon fresh lime juice

TIPS

• This recipe calls for skin-on fish fillets to keep the pieces together, but skinless firm white fish will do.

• Sauté the onions just until barely golden so their flavor is mild and sweet.

• If you don't have Kashmiri chili powder, use a mixture of 3 parts sweet paprika to 1 part cayenne. Make extra and store for future use.

MASALA

When Vasco da Gama arrived in Kerala, he came for the black pepper, but he and the Portuguese fleets that followed ended up introducing fresh chilies and vinegar, which had a lasting impact on the cuisine. We find those two ingredients in a number of dishes—most famously hot and sour vindaloo—but unlike vindaloo, fish molee uses them in a restrained and subtle way. You'll appreciate its perfect burst of acidity from vinegar, lime juice, and tomato, and just the right level of heat from fresh serranos and low-key Kashmiri chili powder. It's a favorite way to eat fish in Kerala. *See photograph on page 170.*

1.   Rinse the fish and pat it dry. Cut it into 3-inch pieces and set it aside.

2.   **Make the tarka:** Assemble your prepped and measured ingredients by the stove. Heat the oil in a deep 10-inch skillet or Dutch oven over medium-high heat until it shimmers. Add the minced ginger, stir for a few seconds, then promptly add the curry leaves and let them crackle until they release their fragrance, which will take just a few seconds. Immediately add the chopped onion, stir, and reduce the heat to medium. Sauté the onion until it is very soft and just beginning to turn golden, 3 to 5 minutes. Add the garlic and green chili and continue to sauté until the garlic smells cooked, another minute or so. Add the turmeric, Kashmiri chili powder, and salt and stir until the spices lose their raw smell, about 1 minute. If they begin to stick to the bottom of the pan, add about 2 tablespoons water and scrape the bottom of the pan with a spatula to loosen them.

3.   **To finish:** Add half of the tomato slices and stir until they begin to soften, 1 minute. Add ½ cup of the coconut milk and the water and continue to stir, scraping the bottom of the pan if necessary, until the ingredients are well blended, about 2 minutes.

4.   Gently add the fish in a single layer, skin-side up. Reduce the heat to low and simmer for 5 minutes. Gently flip the fish and continue to simmer for another 5 minutes, or until the fish is opaque and cooked through. Gently swirl in the remaining ¼ cup coconut milk, the vinegar, and the lime juice and bring just to a simmer. Remove from heat. Discard the green chili, if you wish, then taste for the salt and acidity balance and adjust as needed. Serve immediately in a warmed shallow bowl, garnished with the remaining tomato slices.

CRISPY FISH WITH CURRY LEAF AIOLI

Having grown up in New England, I've long counted fried fish with tartar sauce among my favorite comfort foods. So here's my grown-up take on the combo, blending in Indian flavors to add depth and zest. For the fish batter, I was inspired by the chickpea flour–rice flour batter in snacks like Crispy Kale Pakoras (page 59), because of its rich flavor and crisp texture. And in place of tartar sauce, I love making a fabulous aioli that captures the flavor and fragrance of curry leaves. In this dish, New England meets South India in the most delicious way.

MASALA

FISH

1¼ pounds fillets of sole, flounder, halibut, or cod

½ cup neutral oil, for frying

BATTER

½ cup chickpea flour or besan

¼ cup rice flour

2 tablespoons cornstarch

⅛ teaspoon cayenne

⅛ teaspoon ground turmeric

⅛ teaspoon asafetida (optional)

¼ teaspoon fine sea salt

1 large egg white (reserve yolk for aioli)

½ to ⅔ cup water

CURRY LEAF TARKA

½ cup neutral oil

20 fresh curry leaves (1 inch or longer)

AIOLI

1 (1-inch) cube of unpeeled ginger

1 tablespoon fresh lime juice, plus more if needed

1 large egg yolk

½ teaspoon Dijon-style mustard

½ teaspoon fine sea salt, plus more if needed

1 small garlic clove, minced

1 teaspoon minced serrano or jalapeño

⅓ cup chopped cilantro leaves and tender stems

1. **Prepare the fish:** Rinse the fish fillets and cut them on the diagonal into 2-inch strips. Refrigerate.

2. **Make the batter:** In a medium bowl, combine the flours, cornstarch, cayenne, turmeric, asafetida (if using), salt, egg white, and ½ cup of the water and whisk them together until smooth. Set aside.

3. **Make the curry leaf tarka:** Use caution in this step as the hot oil may sputter out of the pan. In a 10-inch skillet, heat the oil until shimmering. Drop in 1 leaf to make sure it immediately crackles, and if not, continue heating the oil. Carefully and quickly drop the leaves into the oil and step back. After they crackle and start to turn crisp, immediately remove the pan from the heat. Scoop out the curry leaves with a slotted spoon and set them aside to drain on a paper towel. Cool the oil completely and reserve.

4. **Prepare the aioli:** First make the ginger juice by grating the ginger on a Microplane or fine grater onto a plate. Press the gratings through a fine-mesh strainer set over a small bowl to extract 1 teaspoon of ginger juice. Whisk the lime juice, egg yolk, mustard, and salt into the ginger juice to combine.

recipe continues

- If you happen to overcook your curry leaves and they turn brown, discard them and the oil into an empty can or heatproof container you can throw out when cooled—not the sink—and start over.

- The aioli is best eaten within a day or two.

- Garnish with cilantro stems or serve with lime wedges, if you like.

- Serve this with mashed potatoes and Green Bean, Corn, and Coconut Thoren (page 124).

- If you have leftover aioli, you can use it on a sandwich, spoon it over steamed or roasted vegetables, or spoon it into a baked potato. Or make it expressly as a dip for raw vegetables.

5. Transfer the mixture to a mini food processor or blender. Add the garlic, green chili, and cilantro and pulse several times to combine. Check that the reserved curry leaf oil is completely cool. With the motor running, slowly add all the oil in a very thin stream until the mixture is thick and fully emulsified. Add the curry leaves (reserving one or two for garnish) and process until thoroughly combined into the aioli. If you want a thicker aioli, simply add more oil, or to thin it, add a few drops of water. Taste for seasoning and adjust with more lime juice or salt. Transfer to a small serving bowl, garnish with the reserved curry leaves, cover, and refrigerate until ready to serve.

6. Line a large plate with paper towels or brown paper bags.

7. To fry the fish, heat ½ cup oil in a 10-inch skillet (to a depth of about ⅓ inch) over medium-high heat. Remove the fish from the refrigerator. If the batter is very thick, thin it with 1 to 2 tablespoons water. When the oil is shimmering, dip a piece of fish into the batter to coat it completely and place in the oil. Repeat with as many pieces as will fit without crowding the skillet. Cook until the fish is golden on one side, 2 to 3 minutes. Carefully flip the fish and cook until golden, 1 to 2 minutes, then transfer to the lined plate. Continue with the remaining fish until all is cooked.

8. Transfer the fish to a warmed serving platter and serve immediately with the aioli.

KERALA RED FISH CURRY

The tropical state of Kerala has a long coastline and a massive network of rivers and lakes, so naturally it offers many fabulous fish curries. This is one of the most famous, with signature regional ingredients: tart tamarind, bittersweet fenugreek seeds, and bright but mild red chili powder, all blended into bold harmony. For the best flavor, make this dish a few hours ahead and warm it through just before serving.

1½ pounds swordfish steaks or other firm white fish

TAMARIND

1 teaspoon tamarind paste or concentrate

2 tablespoons warm water

TARKA

2 tablespoons neutral oil

½ teaspoon brown or black mustard seeds

¼ teaspoon fenugreek seeds

12 to 15 fresh curry leaves (1 inch or longer; optional but ideal)

2 large shallots, thinly sliced crosswise (1 cup)

1 large garlic clove, minced (1½ teaspoons)

1½ teaspoons minced ginger

2 serranos or jalapeños, split lengthwise with tops intact

1 tablespoon ground coriander

¼ teaspoon ground turmeric

¾ teaspoon Kashmiri chili powder (see Tip)

⅛ teaspoon cayenne

1 large fresh tomato, diced (1½ cups)

1 tablespoon tomato paste

1 teaspoon fine sea salt, plus more to taste

½ cup water

MASALA

TIP

If you don't have Kashmiri chili powder, use a mixture of 3 parts sweet paprika to 1 part cayenne.

SERVING

Serve with Toasted Coconut Rice (page 186) and garlicky green beans.

1. Rinse the fish, trim off the skin, and cut it into 1½-inch chunks. Set aside.

2. **Dilute the tamarind:** In a small bowl, stir together the tamarind paste and warm water until dissolved. Set aside.

3. **Make the tarka:** Assemble your prepped and measured ingredients by the stove. In a Dutch oven or 10-inch sauté pan with a lid, heat the oil over medium high. Add the mustard seeds and allow them to pop, occasionally swirling the pan. After they have popped for a few seconds, add the fenugreek and stir a few more seconds until they brown. Next, add the curry leaves and let them crackle for a few seconds, then add the shallots and reduce the heat to medium. Stir frequently until they soften and begin to brown on the edges, 3 to 5 minutes. Add the garlic, ginger, and green chili and stir for a minute, until fragrant. Add the coriander, turmeric, Kashmiri chili powder, and cayenne and stir for 30 to 60 seconds, until they lose their raw smell (add a little water if they start to stick to the pan). Add the tomato, tomato paste, salt, and water and stir frequently until the tomato breaks down and begins to form a paste, about 3 minutes.

4. Give the tamarind water a good stir and add it to the pan, stirring for 2 minutes to allow the flavors to meld. Place the fish pieces in the sauce in a single layer. Carefully spoon the sauce over the pieces and give the pan a gentle swirl to circulate the sauce. Bring to a simmer over medium heat, then reduce the heat to low. Partially cover and let the fish cook, undisturbed, until just opaque, 8 to 10 minutes. Without stirring, periodically swirl the pan to circulate the sauce and spoon the sauce over the fish. Remove from the heat. (This dish may be prepared in advance up to this point and rewarmed; the flavors will deepen nicely.)

5. Taste for salt and serve immediately.

RICE, NOODLES, AND BREAD

Rice may seem like the predictable accompaniment to your main dish, but it can be a star in its own right. In this chapter I show you how to give rice a big flavor upgrade with a few spices, a touch of ghee, and a little browning in the pan. I guarantee you'll get your guests' attention with the Tamil Lemon Rice (page 183), Toasted Coconut Rice (page 186), and Yogurt Rice with Mustard Seeds (page 189) recipes in this chapter.

Surprised to find noodles here? It just so happens that Indians love them! And since we North Americans adore them, too, this chapter brings the tarka treatment and more to our beloved pasta in Golden Noodles with Tarka Crunch (page 190) and Chandran's Tangy Mee Goreng (page 193).

As for the Garlic Naan (page 194) and Tender Chapatis (page 197), well, who doesn't love Indian flatbreads? The recipes are simple. They take some time to roll and cook, but when you've done that, they are so worth it.

Cooking rice is a paradox: Despite it seeming like a basic process, so many people—capable cooks among them—can't nail it. The key to doing it well requires getting three things exactly right: the rice-to-water ratio, the timing, and the heat. Rice cookers remove some of the mystery, but if you're making it on the stovetop, you need a pot with a tight-fitting lid. And the cardinal rule is you *cannot lift the lid* once you start the cooking process, but you won't need to if you follow these guidelines.

The two types of rice used in this book are long-grain Asian varieties: basmati from India and Pakistan and jasmine from Thailand. Both use essentially the same "absorption" method, with some minor variations.

BASMATI

- *1 part rice to 1½ parts water*
- *Total cooking and resting time: 30 minutes*
- *Serves 4*

1. Rinse 1⅓ cups basmati rice in a large bowl of water by swishing it around and changing the water until it is no longer cloudy. Drain it completely in a fine-mesh strainer.

2. In a medium saucepan with a tight-fitting lid, combine the rice with 2 cups water and ½ teaspoon fine sea salt.

3. Bring it to a full boil over high heat, then reduce the heat to very low, cover tightly, and cook for 20 minutes undisturbed.

4. Remove the pan from the heat, leaving the lid on, and let it rest for 10 minutes.

5. Remove the lid and fluff the rice with a fork to separate the grains.

JASMINE

- *1 part rice to 1¼ parts water*
- *Total cooking and resting time: 22 minutes*
- *Serves 4*

1. In a medium saucepan with a tight-fitting lid, combine 1¼ cups dry, unrinsed jasmine rice, 1½ cups water, and ½ teaspoon fine sea salt.

2. Bring it to a boil over high heat, reduce the heat to very low, cover tightly, and cook for 12 minutes, undisturbed.

3. Remove the pan from the heat, leaving the lid on, and let it rest for 10 minutes.

4. Remove the lid and fluff the rice with a fork to separate the grains.

Opposite: Scented Turmeric Rice (page 187)

BASMATI WITH SHALLOTS AND CUMIN

1⅓ cups basmati rice

TARKA

1 tablespoon ghee, store-bought or homemade (page 232)

1 teaspoon cumin seeds

1 medium shallot, thinly sliced crosswise

½ teaspoon fine sea salt

2 cups water

TIPS

• Always rinse your basmati rice! It removes excess starch and results in grains that are separate and delicate.

• Replace the ghee with any neutral-tasting oil to make it vegan.

SERVING

Pair this rice with any dal, Comforting Chickpeas and Potatoes (page 146), or Classic Saag with Crispy Paneer (page 110).

My husband likes "rice with interest," so this is one of my go-to recipes for quick rice with personality. Each of the four main ingredients—basmati, ghee, cumin, and shallots—contributes to its beautiful aroma. Everyone needs a rice dish like this up their sleeve, because it always fits, no matter how simple or fancy your meal. *See photograph on page 184.*

1. Place the rice in a medium bowl and run cool water over it. When the bowl is two-thirds full, swish the rice with your hand for a minute to loosen the starch. Pour it through a fine-mesh strainer and set aside to drain completely.

2. **Make the tarka:** Assemble your prepped and measured ingredients by the stove. In a 3-quart saucepan with a tight-fitting lid, melt the ghee over medium heat. Add the cumin seeds and, when they sizzle, add the shallot and fry until it turns light brown and fragrant, 3 to 5 minutes.

3. Add the drained rice and stir until the rice is thoroughly coated in ghee. Add the salt and water and bring to a boil over high heat. Reduce the heat to very low, cover tightly, and cook undisturbed for 20 minutes.

4. After 20 minutes, remove the pan from the heat and allow the rice to sit without removing the lid for another 10 minutes to finish steaming. Fluff the rice with a fork and serve. You may keep the rice warm in a low oven, covered, for up to 1 hour.

TAMIL LEMON RICE

There are myriad rice preparations in India, but some of the most flavorful ones come from Tamil Nadu. This one is inspired by our friend Yoga, who is a great Tamil cook. By utilizing the tarka technique to layer in lemon, herbs, spices, and vegetables, the recipe boasts great flavors and textures. It always gets lots of compliments, and it's good served at room temperature, making it perfect for bringing to a party. *See photograph on page 184.*

RICE

1¼ cups jasmine rice

1½ cups water

½ teaspoon fine sea salt, plus more to taste

TARKA

¼ cup neutral oil

1 teaspoon brown or black mustard seeds

2 dried red chilies, or ⅛ teaspoon dried red chili flakes

12 to 15 fresh curry leaves (1 inch or longer; optional but ideal)

1 tablespoon white urad dal or red lentils (masoor dal)

1 medium yellow onion, chopped into ½-inch dice (about 1 cup)

½ red bell pepper, chopped into ½-inch pieces

2 teaspoons minced ginger

½ teaspoon ground turmeric

⅛ teaspoon asafetida (optional)

¾ teaspoon fine sea salt

¼ cup fresh lemon juice, or more to taste, to finish

TIPS

• I prefer jasmine rice because the grains are sturdier than basmati. If using basmati, follow the guidelines on page 180.

• White urad dal is sold at Indian grocery stores, and it adds a nutty crunch to this dish.

SERVING

Pair this with Kerala Red Fish Curry (page 177) or any fish.

1. **Cook the rice:** In a 3-quart saucepan with a tight-fitting lid, bring the rice, water, and salt to a boil over high heat. Reduce the heat to very low and cover tightly. Cook, undisturbed, for 15 minutes (resist the temptation to lift the lid!). Remove the pan from the heat and let sit undisturbed for 10 minutes, then fluff the rice with a fork and replace the lid to keep it warm.

2. **Make the tarka:** While the rice is resting, assemble your prepped and measured ingredients by the stove. Heat the oil in a wok or deep sauté pan (large enough to hold all the rice) over medium-high heat. Add the mustard seeds and allow them to pop, occasionally swirling the pan. After they have popped for a few seconds, add the red chilies and curry leaves and let them crackle for a few seconds. Immediately add the urad dal and sauté for a minute until it begins to turn beige. Then add the onion and bell pepper and sauté until the vegetables are tender but not brown, 5 to 8 minutes. Next, add the ginger, turmeric, asafetida (if using), and salt and sauté for 1 to 2 minutes to meld all the flavors and mellow the raw smell of the turmeric.

3. Remove the pan from the heat and stir in the lemon juice. Add the warm cooked rice and stir gently until the rice is completely golden and the ingredients are combined. Taste for salt and lemon. Serve warm or at room temperature.

Basmati with
Shallots and
Cumin

Tamil
Lemon
Rice

Toasted
Coconut
Rice

TOASTED COCONUT RICE

When it comes to South Indian seasoned rice, the secret lies in the tarka. This is one of the best examples, as it has the warm, earthy aroma of mustard seeds, the crunch of white urad dal, and the sweetness of coconut all stirred together in a heavenly tarka. The key to its perfection is deeply toasting the coconut and cooking the urad dal until just golden. *See photograph on page 185.*

RICE

1¼ cups jasmine rice

½ cup canned full-fat coconut milk

1 cup water

½ teaspoon fine sea salt

TARKA

1 tablespoon unrefined coconut oil

½ teaspoon brown or black mustard seeds

2 dried red chilies, or ⅛ teaspoon dried red chili flakes

10 fresh curry leaves (1 inch or longer; optional)

1 tablespoon white urad dal or red lentils (masoor dal)

¼ cup dried unsweetened shredded coconut

TIPS

• This is a perfect dish for using up leftover coconut milk.

• Garnish this with toasted, chopped cashews to dress it up.

• This has the most fragrance and flavor when warm, but it can also be served at room temperature.

SERVING

• Serve alongside Fish Molee with Fresh Tomato and Coconut (page 172) and Chopped Kachumber Salad (page 82).

• This is a nice summery dish for a barbecue, and it is delicious with any seafood.

1. **Make the rice:** In a medium saucepan, combine the rice, coconut milk, water, and salt and bring to a boil over medium-high heat. Reduce the heat to low, cover, and cook undisturbed for 15 minutes. Don't be tempted to check on the rice as it cooks. When the rice is finished, remove the pan from the heat and let it sit for 10 minutes. Fluff the rice and keep it covered while you prepare the tarka.

2. **Make the tarka:** Assemble your prepped and measured ingredients by the stove. Heat the coconut oil in a medium 10-inch skillet over medium-high heat. Add the mustard seeds and allow them to pop, occasionally swirling the pan. After they have popped for a few seconds, add the chilies and the curry leaves, which will sputter loudly. Reduce the heat to medium and promptly add the urad dal, stirring constantly, until the dal begins to turn beige, 1 to 2 minutes. Add the coconut and cook, stirring constantly, until it turns reddish brown, 1 to 2 minutes (watch that it doesn't burn!).

3. Remove from the heat and scrape everything into the rice. Stir to thoroughly combine and serve.

SCENTED TURMERIC RICE

This is my go-to favorite when I want a rice dish that feels very special but is simple to make. The aromas of the cinnamon, clove, and star anise mingle perfectly with the scent of turmeric, and the peas make it so pretty. *See photograph on page 181.*

1⅓ cups basmati rice

TARKA

1 tablespoon neutral oil

1 (3-inch) stick of cinnamon

3 whole cloves

1 star anise

1 bay leaf

¾ cup thinly sliced yellow onion (about 1 medium)

½ teaspoon ground turmeric

⅛ teaspoon freshly ground black pepper

½ teaspoon fine sea salt

2 cups water

½ cup frozen peas, thawed

TIPS

• I like the way the whole spices look in the finished dish, but you can remove them if you're concerned about biting into them.

• You can substitute jasmine for basmati rice here. Simply follow the guidelines on page 180.

• Fry the onion to a pale golden for the sweetest flavor and brightest color in the final dish.

SERVING

• This is delicious with Peppery Beef Curry (page 166) and Garlicky Tarka Broccoli (page 106) or Creamy Black Lentil Dal (page 138) and Tandoori Cauliflower Steaks (page 105).

• Pair with a sumptuous lamb tagine.

1. Rinse the basmati by swishing it around in a large bowl of water. Pour it through a fine-mesh strainer and set aside to drain completely.

2. **Make the tarka:** Assemble your prepped and measured ingredients by the stove. In a 3-quart saucepan with a tight-fitting lid, heat the oil over medium-high heat. When the oil is shimmering, add the cinnamon, cloves, star anise, and bay leaf and stir until fragrant, about 1 minute. Add the onion and stir frequently until translucent and beginning to brown at the edges, 3 to 5 minutes. Add the turmeric, pepper, and salt and stir until fragrant, 30 seconds. Add the rice and the water, stir, and bring to a boil over high heat. Reduce the heat to very low, tightly cover, and cook undisturbed for 20 minutes. Don't peek!

3. Quickly lift the lid, add the peas, and replace the lid. Remove from the heat and let the rice sit for 10 minutes to finish steaming and heat the peas through.

4. Fluff the rice to incorporate the peas before serving and transfer to a warm bowl.

YOGURT RICE WITH MUSTARD SEEDS

In India this dish is known as "curd rice," and it makes South Indians swoon! The texture is a little like risotto, but with savory South Indian ingredients like ginger and green chili in a creamy yogurt base. The tarka brings it all together with nutty flavors and crunchy textures. It is typically served with vegetable curries, but I'm irreverent; I pair it with spicy fish dishes.

RICE

1 cup jasmine rice

1¼ cups water

½ teaspoon fine sea salt

YOGURT

1½ cups plain whole milk yogurt (not Greek-style; see Tip)

1 cup milk (preferably whole or 2 percent), plus more for thinning as needed

1 teaspoon minced ginger

1 teaspoon minced serrano, jalapeño, or Thai bird chili

½ teaspoon fine sea salt

TARKA

3 tablespoons neutral oil

1½ teaspoons brown or black mustard seeds

2 dried red chilies, broken in half, or ⅛ teaspoon dried red chili flakes

12 to 15 fresh curry leaves (1 inch or longer)

1 tablespoon white urad dal or red lentils (masoor dal)

⅛ teaspoon asafetida (optional)

TIPS

• You can substitute 1 cup Greek-style yogurt mixed with ½ cup water for the plain yogurt.

• Jasmine absorbs the yogurt better than basmati.

SERVING

• This is wonderful with Red Chili Shrimp (page 169).

• It is great served with achar (pickle) and crisp papadam (lentil wafers).

1. **Prepare the rice:** In a 2-quart saucepan, bring the rice, water, and salt to a boil. Reduce the heat to low, cover tightly, and cook, undisturbed, for 15 minutes. Remove the pan from the heat and let it rest, with the lid on, for another 10 minutes. Spread the rice evenly onto a large baking sheet to cool completely, about 15 minutes at room temperature, or less in the refrigerator. If the rice is warm, it will cause the yogurt to separate.

2. **Mix in the yogurt:** Transfer the cooled rice to a large serving bowl. Add the yogurt, ½ cup of the milk, the ginger, green chili, and salt and mix thoroughly. (At this point, you can set it aside at room temperature or in the refrigerator for up to 1 hour; just know that the rice will continue to absorb moisture as it sits, so you may need to adjust the amount of milk added at the end.)

3. **Make the tarka:** Assemble your prepped and measured ingredients by the stove. Heat the oil in a 10-inch skillet over medium heat. Add the mustard seeds and allow them to pop, occasionally swirling the pan. After they have popped for a few seconds, add the dried chilies and curry leaves and allow them to crackle for a few seconds. Immediately add the urad dal and fry until it begins to turn beige, about 30 seconds. Add the asafetida, if using, and stir for 30 seconds until fragrant, then remove from the heat. Pull out a few of the curry leaves for garnish and pour the rest of the tarka over the rice. Stir to combine well.

4. Mix in the remaining ½ cup milk. The rice should have the texture of soft rice pudding, so add more milk if necessary. Serve cool or at room temperature, topped with the reserved curry leaves.

GOLDEN NOODLES WITH TARKA CRUNCH

There's a wonderful South Indian noodle dish with ginger, green chili, and urad dal called vermicelli upma. It's technically a breakfast dish, but I when I eat it, I see dinner potential! So I've adapted it here with a chili-spiked tarka that makes it a great side dish at any meal. And while I like it as a side dish, it could easily be a main dish for two or three people if you add a protein like pressed tofu.

PASTA

½ pound angel hair pasta

Kosher salt

Neutral oil, for drizzling

TARKA

3 tablespoons neutral oil

1 teaspoon brown or black mustard seeds

¼ teaspoon dried red chili flakes

12 to 15 curry leaves (1 inch or longer), sliced into thin ribbons (optional)

2 teaspoons white urad dal or red lentils (masoor dal)

½ large yellow onion, chopped into ¼-inch dice (1½ cups)

1 whole serrano or 1½ jalapeños, finely chopped

1 (1½-inch) piece of ginger, cut into matchsticks (¼ cup)

¼ teaspoon ground turmeric

½ teaspoon fine sea salt, plus more to taste

TO FINISH

2 tablespoons fresh lemon juice

2 tablespoons chopped cilantro leaves and tender stems

TIP

To make matchsticks, cut the ginger lengthwise into very thin slabs, then stack the slabs and cut them lengthwise again into slivers.

SERVING

Serve in place of rice with a nice juicy curry.

1. **Prepare the pasta:** Grasping a small handful at a time, snap the raw pasta into roughly 2-inch lengths. Set a baking pan near the stove. Heat a wok or large skillet over medium-high heat, add the pasta, and toast it, stirring and shaking the pan, until it is unevenly but distinctively golden, about 3 minutes. Pour the pasta into the baking pan so it doesn't continue to toast or burn.

2. Bring a stockpot of salted water to a boil. Cook the pasta according to the package directions until just cooked through, 2 to 4 minutes—don't overcook. Reserve 1 cup of the pasta water before you drain it into a colander. Drizzle the pasta with a little oil and toss to prevent it from sticking as you prepare the tarka.

3. **Make the tarka:** Assemble your prepped and measured ingredients by the stove. In a wok or 11- to 12-inch skillet, heat the oil over medium heat until it shimmers. Add the mustard seeds and allow them to pop, occasionally swirling the pan. After they have popped for a few seconds, add the chili flakes and the curry leaves, which will sputter loudly. Promptly add the urad dal and cook until it begins to turn beige, 30 to 60 seconds. Quickly add the onion, green chili, and ginger and continue sautéing over medium heat until the onion begins to brown, 3 to 4 minutes. Add the turmeric and salt and sauté until the turmeric loses its raw smell, about 1 minute.

4. Add the pasta to the wok, reduce the heat to medium-low, and stir just until the noodles are warmed through, 1 to 2 minutes. If the pasta seems dry, add a few tablespoons of the reserved pasta water.

5. **To finish:** Remove from the heat and stir in the lemon juice. Taste and adjust the seasoning. Transfer to a warm bowl, top with the cilantro, and serve.

CHANDRAN'S TANGY MEE GORENG

Mee goreng means "fried noodles" in Malay. It likely originated in China, but today it is one of the most popular street foods in Southeast Asia and involves noodles stir-fried with vegetables, egg (or shrimp or meat), and a light soy and vinegar sauce. My grandparents lived in Kuala Lumpur, Malaya (Malaysia now), when my father, Chandran, was little, and my grandmother learned to make this dish there, which is how it became my dad's favorite. My siblings and I loved it when he made these tangy noodles for us. Recently my brother, Narayan, found the recipe on an old index card from the 1970s in my father's neat handwriting, so I had to include it here.

PASTA

Kosher salt

½ pound spaghetti or linguine

Neutral oil, for drizzling

SAUCE

½ cup soy sauce

6 tablespoons white vinegar

1 teaspoon sugar

1 serrano or jalapeño, thinly sliced

EGGS AND VEGETABLES

3 tablespoons plus 1 teaspoon neutral oil

2 large eggs

Fine sea salt

1 large onion, cut into ¼-inch slices, root to stem (2 cups)

¼ pound fresh bean sprouts, or 3 cups thinly sliced green cabbage

½ pound fresh spinach, well washed, tough stems removed, leaves coarsely chopped

5 scallions (white and green parts), coarsely chopped, for garnish

TIP

You can easily make this dish vegan by omitting the egg.

SERVING

• This is a perfect one-dish meal. Top it with chili crisp.

• Skip the egg and serve it with seared marinated tofu.

1. **Cook the pasta:** Bring a pot of salted water to a boil. Cook the pasta according to the package instructions until tender, about 10 minutes. Drain in a colander and toss with a little bit of oil to prevent sticking. Set aside.

2. **Mix the sauce:** In a small bowl, combine the soy sauce, vinegar, sugar, and green chili and set aside.

3. **Prepare the eggs and vegetables:** Heat ½ teaspoon of the oil in a wok or an 11-inch nonstick pan. Whisk 1 of the eggs with a pinch of sea salt in a small bowl and add it to the hot pan. Swirl the pan around so the egg cooks in a uniform thickness, like a crepe. Once it's firm but not dry on top, carefully flip it to briefly cook the other side, then remove it to a cutting board. Repeat with another ½ teaspoon oil and the remaining egg. Stack them on a cutting board and cut each into two half-moons, then stack and cut them into thin ¼-inch strips. Set aside.

4. In the same pan, pour the remaining 3 tablespoons oil, add the onion, and cook over medium-high heat until it begins to soften, stirring frequently. Add the bean sprouts and stir until hot, 2 to 3 minutes. Add the spinach and cook just long enough to wilt it, 2 to 3 minutes more. Add in the pasta and, using tongs or two spatulas, toss and mix everything together until the entire mixture is hot. Toss in the egg strips and combine well.

5. Stir in the prepared sauce and mix completely. Transfer to a warm serving bowl, garnish with the chopped scallions, and serve.

GARLIC NAAN

If you enjoy bread baking, this is an easy recipe to master. I've suggested my favorite toppings, but you can try other herbs and aromatics such as rosemary, mint, red onion—or whatever you fancy!

DOUGH

1 cup warm water

2 teaspoons sugar

1 (0.25-ounce) packet active dry yeast (2¼ teaspoons)

2 tablespoons plain whole-milk yogurt

⅓ cup whole milk

1 teaspoon fine sea salt

3 cups plus 2 tablespoons (435g) unbleached all-purpose flour, plus more for dusting

TOPPINGS

4 teaspoons nigella seeds

4 medium garlic cloves, minced

½ cup chopped cilantro leaves and tender stems

Fine sea salt

Freshly ground black pepper

¼ cup melted ghee, store-bought or homemade (page 232)

SERVING

• Cut naan into strips and serve with Roasted Tomato Tarka with Yogurt (page 64) and Sweet Pea and Cashew Dip with Mint (page 63).

• This pairs well with Classic Saag with Crispy Paneer (page 110).

• Naan is always good for scooping up dal.

1. **Prepare the dough:** Place the water in a large bowl. Stir in the sugar, then the yeast and let sit until the yeast "blooms," creating a foamy layer on the surface of the water, about 10 minutes.

2. Stir in the yogurt, milk, and salt, then slowly add 2¾ cups (340g) of the flour, working it in with your hands (alternatively, you can mix this in a stand mixer with a dough hook). If the mixture is very sticky, add an additional ¼ cup of the flour (or more), 1 tablespoon at a time, until you have a soft, lovely, but still slightly sticky dough.

3. Shape the dough into a ball, place it in a clean bowl, and cover with a dish towel. Turn on your oven to the lowest setting (175°F or 200°F) and when it reaches 100°F, turn off the oven. Place the bowl of dough in the oven and let it rise until doubled in bulk, 1 to 1½ hours.

4. Punch down the dough gently, transfer it to a floured work surface, and cut it into 8 equal-size pieces. Form into balls and let them relax for 15 minutes.

5. Heat a heavy skillet, preferably cast iron, over medium-high heat.

6. **Shape the dough and add the toppings:** Lightly sprinkle your work surface and the surface of the dough with flour and roll out oblong shapes about 8 inches long and ¼ inch thick. If you find the dough is sticking, add more flour as you roll it out. Sprinkle the dough with a generous pinch of each of the toppings and give it a quick roll to cement the toppings into the dough.

7. When the skillet is hot, place the dough, plain-side down, in the skillet. After about 30 seconds, the dough will bubble. Cook until the bottom is very brown with some burnt spots on it, about 2 minutes. Using tongs or your fingers, carefully flip the dough and cook the second side, pressing on it slightly so the dough browns and the toppings cook evenly, 1 to 1½ minutes. Transfer the naan to a serving dish—topping-side up—and brush with melted ghee. Repeat with the remaining dough rounds. (You can serve these as they come out of the pan or keep them warm in the oven as you continue baking.)

TENDER CHAPATIS

2 cups (250g) Indian atta flour (see Tip), plus more for dusting

1 teaspoon fine sea salt

¼ cup plus 1 teaspoon melted ghee, store-bought or homemade (page 232)

¾ to 1¼ cups warm water

TIPS

• Atta (durum wheat flour) is definitely the best flour choice. Also called chapati flour, you can find it at an Indian grocery or online. If you can't locate it, use a mixture of 1⅓ cups (185g) all-purpose flour and ⅔ cup (90g) whole-wheat flour.

• Replace the ghee with neutral oil to make these vegan.

• If you have a tortilla keeper, use it to keep the chapatis warm as you cook them.

SERVING

• These are perfect with Tea-Braised Punjabi Chickpeas (page 145) or Classic Dal Tarka (page 135).

• Use chapatis as wraps with Chicken Tikka Skewers (page 157) or Turkey Keema with Sweet Potatoes (page 158).

Homemade chapatis are lovely, but don't be surprised if it takes you a couple of tries before you're comfortable making them. Practice on your family before you serve them to guests. And consider recruiting a helper to speed up the process and make it more fun—one can roll, the other can cook!

1. In a medium bowl, combine the flour, salt, 1 teaspoon of the melted ghee, and enough water to make a stiff but pliable dough. It should be stiffer than bread dough, but not sticky, and just soft enough to work into a smooth ball, so when you add the water, begin with ¾ cup, adding more by the tablespoon as needed. The dough should hold a finger depression with minimal springback. Knead the dough for about 3 minutes, until it becomes smooth and somewhat elastic. Return it to the bowl, cover with a dish towel, and set aside for 30 minutes to relax.

2. Turn out the dough and form it into a long log. Divide the log into 16 pieces and roll each one into a ball (they should be just shy of Ping-Pong-ball size, about 1½ inches in diameter). Lightly dust a work surface with flour (use atta if you've got it; otherwise you can use all-purpose flour). Roll a ball in flour, then pat the ball into a flat round and roll it out so that it is 4 to 5 inches in diameter and ¹⁄₁₆ inch thick—about the thickness of a flour tortilla. Set it aside on a tray or cutting board and repeat with the remaining dough, overlapping them as you stack, with a sprinkle of flour between each to prevent sticking. Set the tray next to the stove.

3. Heat a heavy frying pan or cast-iron skillet over medium to medium-high heat. When the pan is hot enough to immediately brown a sprinkle of flour, place a disk of dough in the pan, and cook until bubbles form and light brown spots appear on the underside, about 30 seconds. Flip and cook longer, 45 to 60 seconds, until there are medium dark brown spots on the other side. Flip it back to the first side and cook for 20 to 30 seconds, pressing down gently around the edges with a folded paper towel to encourage large air bubbles to form. (Sometimes they puff fully, sometimes partially, sometimes not at all—do what you can!).

4. Remove the cooked chapati to a large dish towel, brush it quickly with ghee, and keep it wrapped up as you continue to cook all of the chapatis. Serve warm.

SWEET BITES

What's the perfect sweet bite to have after an Indian meal?
Traditional Indian sweets are wonderful, but I dream of
ways to bring Indian flavors to Western-style desserts and
offer that special hint of the subcontinent in unexpected but
familiar ways. The recipes in this chapter do just that: they
are the result of years of experimentation that I'm excited to
share with you.

In these recipes, I lean into deep flavors like dark
chocolate, coffee, and caramel but also feature fruit like
dates, orange marmalade, and roasted pineapple. There
are Nigella Butter Cookies (page 201) that beg to be eaten
with a cup of chai, a rich Chocolate Tart with Cashew Crust
(page 210) that demands a drumroll, and a sumptuous
Toasted Coconut Rice Pudding (page 205) you can sink into.
And throughout the chapter I've made frequent use of Kerala
Garam Masala (page 224), the warm, sweet spice blend that
works equally well in sweet and savory dishes, as well as notes
of cardamom, nigella seeds, and saffron. My goal is to make
these sweets the ideal conclusion to a meal, with the perfect
indulgence you love and the hint of unique flavor you crave.

SPICY GINGERSNAPS

1½ sticks (180g) unsalted butter, at room temperature

1 cup (200g) packed dark brown sugar

¼ cup molasses

1 large egg

4 teaspoons freshly grated ginger (a Microplane works well for this)

2½ cups (390g) all-purpose flour

½ teaspoon baking powder

½ teaspoon fine sea salt

4 teaspoons North Indian garam masala, store-bought or homemade (page 222)

¼ to ½ teaspoon cayenne, to taste

½ teaspoon ground ginger

¼ cup granulated sugar, for rolling

A true East-meets-West cookie, this recipe is based on my mother's gingersnaps from my childhood and made with my father's garam masala spice blend. To give them extra zing, I add freshly grated ginger and a hit of cayenne. It's fun to use Indian woodblocks to stamp them out if you happen to have any—I got the idea from the talented dessert queen Hetal Vasavada. But any cookie stamp will work, or use a potato masher, a meat mallet, or a fork—so many options! *See photograph on page 203.*

1. In the large bowl of a stand mixer with a paddle attachment, cream the butter until fluffy on medium-high speed. (Alternatively, you can use a large bowl and a hand mixer.) Add the brown sugar and molasses and mix on medium for a few minutes, then add the egg and fresh ginger and blend until well mixed and light.

2. In a medium bowl, combine the flour, baking powder, salt, garam masala, cayenne to taste, and ground ginger. Gradually add the flour mixture to the butter–brown sugar mixture until well blended.

3. Gather the dough into two balls and wrap them in plastic wrap, flattening them slightly to form fat disks. Chill for 30 to 45 minutes, until stiff—this will make the dough easier to handle and stamp.

4. When the dough has chilled, remove one of the disks, keeping the other refrigerated.

5. Preheat the oven to 375°F.

6. Place the granulated sugar in a small bowl. Line two large baking sheets with parchment paper. Tear off tablespoon-size pieces of dough, rolling them between your palms into 1-inch-diameter balls. Roll each ball in the granulated sugar to coat completely and place them on the prepared baking sheets about 2 inches apart. Stamp each cookie with the press of your choice to a ¼-inch thickness. If you find your stamp sticks, dip it in granulated sugar between cookies. The cookies should now be about ½ inch from each other. Continue with the remaining dough, then bake until the cookies are golden and have puffed slightly, 9 to 12 minutes. If the cookies are baked for 9 minutes, you'll get the chewy effect; at 12 minutes, they'll be tender. Transfer the cookies to a wire rack to cool completely. Store the cookies in an airtight container at room temperature for up to 1 week.

NIGELLA BUTTER COOKIES

2½ cups (390g) all-purpose flour

½ cup (100g) granulated sugar

⅛ teaspoon fine sea salt

¼ teaspoon ground turmeric

1¾ sticks unsalted butter (200g), cool but malleable, cut into chunks

1 large egg plus 1 large egg yolk (reserve white for rolling)

½ teaspoon vanilla extract

¼ cup coarse sugar, such as turbinado, raw, or sanding sugar

1 tablespoon nigella seeds (kalonji) or black sesame seeds

These little, not-too-sweet cookies are based on a sweet short-crust Italian pastry called pasta frolla. I learned about it from my dear friend and cookbook author Susan Herrmann Loomis, who was the inspiration for this recipe (and many others). So while the cookies are European in origin, these feature a little Indian drama with turmeric and nigella seeds. Nigella (also called kalonji) are matte black seeds with a perfumy note found in Indian breads and the fragrant seed mix Panch Phoron (page 226). So if you've got nigella seeds sitting in your spice cupboard, this is a great chance to use them. And if you don't, you could substitute black sesame seeds, but the flavor will not be as Indian. *See photograph on page 203.*

1.   Place the flour, granulated sugar, salt, and turmeric in a food processor and pulse to mix. Add the butter and pulse until the mixture is crumbly and nearly holds together. Add the whole egg and the yolk and the vanilla and pulse until the dough is homogeneous.

2.   Divide the dough in half and roll each piece into a log about 1 inch in diameter. Wrap in parchment and chill for an hour, or until firm.

3.   Preheat the oven to 375°F. Line two large baking sheets with parchment paper.

4.   Place the coarse sugar and the nigella seeds in a small bowl and mix well. In another small bowl, whisk the reserved egg white until a little frothy. Working on a piece of parchment, lay down one log, brush it completely with egg white, then sprinkle it with the sugar-nigella mixture. Roll the log, sprinkling it with more of the sugar-nigella mixture, until it is completely encrusted. Slice the cookies crosswise ¼ inch thick and set them on the prepared baking sheets, leaving about an inch between cookies. Repeat with the second log. Bake for 10 to 12 minutes, until golden brown on the bottom. Rest for 5 minutes, then remove the cookies to a rack to cool. When completely cool, store the cookies in an airtight container at room temperature for up to 1 week.

Chocolate
Pistachio
Shortbread

Spicy Gingersnaps

Nigella Butter
Cookies

CHOCOLATE PISTACHIO SHORTBREAD

In my constant search for fine little sweets to accompany my afternoon tea, these, with their garam masala perfume, have become favorites. *See photograph on page 202.*

DOUGH

1¾ sticks (200g) unsalted butter, cut into small pieces, at room temperature

¾ cup (95g) confectioners' sugar

1 large egg, lightly beaten

1½ cups (200g) all-purpose flour, plus more for dusting

6 tablespoons (40g) unsweetened cocoa

1½ teaspoons Kerala Garam Masala (see page 224)

¼ teaspoon fine sea salt

¼ teaspoon baking powder

GARNISH

5 ounces (150g) white chocolate, coarsely chopped

½ cup (75g) unsalted pistachios, chopped medium-fine

2 tablespoons dried rose petals, crumbled (optional)

TIP

You can shape the dough logs and wrap them in plastic wrap, to pull out and bake as you like. The logs will keep for 2 days in the refrigerator and 2 months in the freezer. If frozen, thaw the dough for 30 minutes at room temperature before slicing and baking.

1. **Prepare the dough:** In the bowl of a stand mixer with a paddle attachment, mix the butter on medium-high speed until it is soft and pale yellow. (Alternatively, you can use a large bowl and hand mixer.) Add the confectioners' sugar and continue to mix on medium-high until well mixed and fluffy. Add the egg and mix until blended.

2. Sift the flour, cocoa, garam masala, salt, and baking powder into a medium bowl. Gradually add it to the butter-sugar mixture, blending well.

3. Turn the dough out onto a lightly floured surface and divide it into 3 pieces. Roll each piece into a log that measures about 1¼ × 7 inches. Wrap each log in plastic wrap and refrigerate for at least 2 hours and up to 2 days.

4. Preheat the oven to 425°F and arrange a rack in the center. Line two large baking sheets with parchment paper.

5. Cut the chilled logs into ¼-inch-thick rounds and set them on the prepared baking sheet, leaving about ½ inch between each. Bake in the center of the oven until they are firm and slightly puffed, 7 to 8 minutes. Remove from the oven and promptly transfer the cookies to wire racks to cool. Repeat with the remaining dough.

6. **Prepare the garnish:** Fill a medium saucepan with 1 inch of water and set a medium heatproof bowl on top. When the cookies have cooled, place the chocolate in the bowl. Bring the water to a boil, then simmer over the lowest possible heat until the chocolate appears half melted, 1 to 2 minutes. Remove from the heat and set it aside, uncovered, to continue to melt from the residual heat in the pan. Whisk until completely smooth. Place the pistachios and the rose petals in two small bowls. Dip half of each cookie into the white chocolate, then the pistachios. Set them on a wire rack. Sprinkle each cookie with a pinch of rose petals and let the chocolate cool and harden. Store the cookies in an airtight container at room temperature for up to 10 days.

TOASTED COCONUT RICE PUDDING

4 cups whole milk, plus more as needed

½ cup jasmine rice

½ cup sugar

¼ teaspoon vanilla extract

½ teaspoon fine sea salt

⅓ cup dried unsweetened shredded coconut

½ cup full-fat canned coconut milk

⅓ cup dried currants or raisins

TIPS

• Stir the cooking rice regularly to avoid it sticking to the bottom of the pan and boiling over.

• This pudding is best served warm. If you prepare it ahead, re-warm it and make the garnish just before serving.

India has many elegant rice puddings known as kheer in the north and payasam in the south, made with saffron, cardamom, nuts, and fruits. This one, created with the help of my friend and product development chef Jessica Bard, is more like a comforting American rice pudding with a heady hit of toasted coconut.

1. Place the milk in a medium saucepan over medium-high heat. Stir in the rice, sugar, vanilla, and salt, and bring the mixture to a near-boil. Immediately reduce the heat to low so the milk is just simmering and cook, stirring periodically so the rice doesn't stick to the bottom of the pan, until the rice is tender, about 30 minutes. It should have a somewhat loose consistency because it will continue to thicken as it sits off the heat.

2. While the rice is cooking, toast the coconut in a small skillet over medium heat, stirring frequently, until it is pecan brown and fills the kitchen with a lovely aroma, 3 to 5 minutes. Pour the coconut onto a plate to stop it from toasting.

3. When the rice is cooked, remove it from the heat and stir in the coconut milk, currants, and all but 1 tablespoon of the toasted coconut. Set aside until ready to serve. (You can prepare the pudding 2 hours ahead of time up to this point and leave it at room temperature.)

4. When you're ready to serve, the pudding should be lukewarm or at room temperature. If it seems too thick, add a little milk to thin it. Serve in bowls sprinkled with the remaining tablespoon of toasted coconut.

MARMALADE SAFFRON SQUARES

My father loved orange marmalade, so I definitely had him in mind when I developed these bars. They combine English-style shortbread and marmalade with Indian saffron and garam masala, and the result is a sweet blend of cultures.

DOUGH

2¼ cups (320g) all-purpose flour

½ teaspoon fine sea salt

1½ teaspoons Kerala Garam Masala (page 224)

2 sticks (250g) unsalted butter, softened

⅓ cup (65g) granulated sugar

⅓ cup (70g) packed light brown sugar

1 large egg yolk

¾ teaspoon vanilla extract

FRUIT LAYER

¼ teaspoon (or a generous pinch) saffron threads

2 tablespoons heavy cream

¾ cup bitter orange marmalade (see Tip)

TIP

For this recipe you can use British marmalade, which is dark, thick, and pleasantly bitter, or a French marmalade like Bonne Maman, which is more liquidy and less bitter.

SERVING

Serve with saffron tea made with boiled water, a few saffron threads, and a touch of honey.

1. Preheat the oven to 350°F. Line a 9-inch square pan with parchment paper, leaving an overhang on two opposite sides.

2. **Make the dough:** Combine the flour, salt, and garam masala in a medium bowl and whisk together.

3. Place the butter in the bowl of a stand mixer with the paddle attachment and beat until soft and light. (Alternatively, use a large bowl and a hand mixer.) Add the granulated and brown sugars and cream together until combined. Add the egg yolk and the vanilla and mix thoroughly.

4. With the mixer on low speed, add the dry ingredients slowly and mix until just combined, scraping the bowl several times during mixing. The dough will be thick and sort of lumpy but easy to handle.

5. Set aside about a quarter of the dough for the topping. Press the remaining dough into the bottom of the prepared pan as evenly as you can. Bake in the center of the oven until the edges are lightly browned, about 25 minutes. Remove from the oven and let cool.

6. **Prepare the fruit layer:** While the crust is cooling, crumble the saffron into the cream in a small saucepan and set it over low heat until the cream is hot. Set aside for 15 minutes to let the saffron release its color. Mix in the marmalade and stir until combined.

7. When both the crust and the mixture are cool, spread the fruit layer over the cooled pastry. Crumble the remaining dough over the marmalade, letting some of it show through.

8. Return the pan to the oven and bake until the crust is golden and baked through, another 35 minutes. Remove from the oven and let cool thoroughly. Lift the pastry out using the parchment overhang and set on a cutting board. Cut into 16 squares and serve. These will keep in an airtight container at room temperature for 1 week.

RICH CARROT COCONUT CAKE

A decadently moist cake with a coconut aroma, this is a refreshing change from traditional carrot cakes. Coconut oil is the key to the richness of this scrumptious cake, while the delicate lemon glaze provides the perfect bright counterpoint.

CAKE

1 cup (225g) unrefined coconut oil, melted, plus more for the pan (see Tip)

2 cups (300g) all-purpose flour, plus more for the pan

Pinch of fine sea salt

1½ teaspoons baking powder

1 teaspoon baking soda

2 teaspoons ground cardamom

1½ cups (300g) granulated sugar

5 large eggs

½ cup whole milk

3 large carrots, trimmed and grated (3 generous cups)

2 cups (180g) dried unsweetened shredded coconut

GLAZE

1¼ cups (150g) confectioners' sugar

2 tablespoons whole milk

1 tablespoon fresh lemon juice

TIPS

• If you don't have a Bundt pan, use an oiled and floured 9 × 13-inch baking pan, and start checking if a sharp knife comes out clean at 35 minutes. It should take 35 to 45 minutes to bake.

• Be sure your coconut oil is unrefined (labeled virgin or extra-virgin) for the best flavor.

• This can easily be made dairy-free by substituting a nondairy milk.

1. Preheat the oven to 350°F. Lightly coat an 8-cup Bundt pan with coconut oil and flour.

2. **Prepare the cake:** In a large bowl, sift together the flour, salt, baking powder, baking soda, and cardamom.

3. In the bowl of a stand mixer fitted with the paddle attachment, whisk together the coconut oil and granulated sugar on medium speed until creamy. (Alternatively, you can use a large bowl and a hand mixer.) Add the eggs, one at a time, and mix on medium-high until thoroughly combined. Fold in the dry ingredients a third at a time, alternating with the milk and beginning and ending with the dry ingredients. Fold in the carrots and the shredded coconut.

4. Pour the batter into the prepared pan and bake in the center of the oven until the cake is puffed and golden and a sharp knife inserted into the center comes out with little crumbs sticking to it, 40 to 50 minutes.

5. Transfer the cake to a cooling rack. Unmold the cake onto the rack when it is still warmish and let it cool entirely.

6. **Make the glaze:** While the cake is cooling, in a medium bowl whisk together the confectioners' sugar, milk, and lemon juice. When the cake is completely cool, place it on a cake plate and drizzle the glaze over the top before serving. This cake keeps well, covered at room temperature, for several days.

CHOCOLATE TART WITH CASHEW CRUST

This gem is inspired by a mocha tart from baker and cookbook author Alice Medrich, only transported to India via cashews and Kerala garam masala. It's delicious, easy, and gorgeous.

CRUST

½ cup (75g) unsalted roasted cashews

¼ cup (50g) sugar

1 cup (140g) all-purpose flour, plus more for dusting

½ teaspoon fine sea salt

1 teaspoon Kerala Garam Masala (page 224)

7 tablespoons (105g) unsalted butter, cut into chunks, at room temperature

FILLING

3 tablespoons (45g) unsalted butter, cut into ½-inch cubes

½ cup (100g) sugar

¼ cup (25g) best-quality cocoa powder

1 cup heavy cream

¼ teaspoon Kerala Garam Masala (page 224)

½ teaspoon vanilla extract

1 large egg, lightly beaten

GARNISH (OPTIONAL)

1 cup heavy cream

1 teaspoon sugar

½ cup unsalted roasted cashews, coarsely chopped

TIPS

• You will need a 9½-inch fluted tart pan with a removable bottom, or a 9-inch pie pan.

• The pastry *must be hot* and the filling *must be warm* when you combine them, so bake the pastry and make the filling simultaneously.

1. Preheat the oven to 350°F.

2. **Make the crust:** Finely grind the cashews and sugar in a food processor. Add the flour, salt, and garam masala and process for 5 seconds. Add the butter and pulse until well blended. It's a soft dough and won't adhere in one ball, but don't worry.

3. Using your flour-dusted fingers, press the dough into a 9½-inch fluted tart pan with a removable bottom in an even layer across the bottom and up the sides. Don't be concerned if it isn't perfectly flat, as imperfections bake out. Bake until pale golden, 20 to 25 minutes.

4. **While the crust is baking, prepare the filling:** In a 3-quart saucepan over medium heat, place the butter, sugar, cocoa powder, cream, and garam masala, and as the butter begins to melt, slowly whisk the ingredients together. When small bubbles appear at the edges of the liquid and it is smooth, remove the pan from the heat. Whisk in the vanilla and then the egg.

5. As soon as the crust is baked, remove it from the oven and promptly turn off the oven.

6. Pour the filling into the hot baked crust. Return it to the oven and allow it to set in the residual heat for 15 to 20 minutes, or until it has a firm but slightly jiggly consistency. Transfer to a cooling rack. If for some reason the filling fails to set, turn on the oven to 350°F while the tart is still in the oven and check it every 5 minutes.

7. **Make the garnish, if desired:** Using an electric mixer, whip the cream and sugar until firm peaks form, about 7 minutes. Refrigerate until ready to serve.

8. When cool enough to handle, remove the tart from the pan and serve it warm or cool, with the whipped cream and topped with the cashews (if using). This tart will keep for a few days covered at room temperature.

CARAMELIZED SPICED PINEAPPLE WITH WHIPPED COCONUT CREAM

WHIPPED COCONUT CREAM

1 (14-ounce) can full-fat coconut milk (chilled; see Tip, below)

1 teaspoon granulated sugar

¼ teaspoon vanilla extract

TOASTED COCONUT

¼ cup (18g) dried unsweetened shredded coconut

PINEAPPLE

1 ripe pineapple (1¾ pounds), peeled (see Tip, page 214)

2 tablespoons ghee, store-bought or homemade (page 232), or unsalted butter

½ teaspoon ground ginger

¼ teaspoon ground cinnamon

Pinch of ground cloves

¼ teaspoon ground cardamom

⅓ cup (75g) firmly packed dark brown sugar

TIP

Note that you will need *organic* coconut milk with no additives or emulsifiers for this recipe. To separate the fat from the watery liquid, the unopened can needs to chill for 3 hours or up to overnight, prior to being whipped—but do not put it in the freezer.

This recipe was inspired by Susan Westmoreland, my friend and the food director of *Good Housekeeping* magazine when I worked there. Susan has a passion for Indian food, and I enjoy the way she brings Indian flavors into her own cooking, as in this chai spice–laced dessert.

1. **Prepare the whipped coconut cream:** Open the can of chilled coconut milk and carefully scoop out the solidified fat (reserving the watery portion in the can) and place it in the bowl of a stand mixer. (Alternatively, you can use a medium bowl and hand mixer.) Add the granulated sugar, vanilla, and 1 tablespoon of the reserved liquid in the can. Whip it on high until it holds soft peaks. Don't expect it to be as voluminous as whipped cream. If it seems too stiff, add more of the coconut water, a teaspoon at a time. Cover and refrigerate. Discard the excess liquid. (This can be done several hours in advance, or even the night before.)

2. **Toast the coconut:** Put the shredded coconut in an 8-inch skillet over medium heat. Stir constantly until the flakes become a nice toasty orangish-brown color, 3 to 5 minutes. Don't leave the skillet, as the coconut can burn quickly. Transfer the toasted coconut to a plate to immediately stop the browning. Set aside for the garnish. Wipe the skillet clean for later use.

3. **Prepare the pineapple:** Line a large baking sheet with aluminum foil. Cut the peeled pineapple lengthwise into quarters. Slice out the tough core, then cut each quarter into 3 long wedges. Arrange the pineapple wedges on the foil.

4. Preheat the broiler and arrange the rack 4 inches from the heat source.

5. Place the skillet you used for toasting the coconut over medium heat and add the ghee to melt. Stir in the ground spices and let them cook and bubble for 1 minute. Remove the pan from the heat.

recipe continues

• To peel the pineapple, cut off the crown and base. Stand the pineapple on the base end and slice down, cutting off the rind and "eyes." There will still be some deep eyes in the pineapple, which you can either leave in or cut out with a paring knife or the end of a swivel vegetable peeler.

• This entire dish can be prepared ahead of time and assembled right before serving.

6. Brush the tops of each pineapple wedge with half of the spiced ghee. Divide half of the brown sugar among the wedges, patting equal amounts onto each one. Some sugar will fall off, but don't be concerned. Broil the pineapple wedges until golden and beginning to caramelize at the edges, 3 to 5 minutes.

7. Remove the baking sheet from the oven and, using tongs, flip the pineapple wedges and brush them with the remaining spiced ghee. Pat equal amounts of the remaining brown sugar onto the pineapple. Return to the broiler and broil until the pineapple begins to caramelize, 3 to 4 additional minutes. Transfer the pineapple to a platter and set aside so it cools to room temperature. (This may be prepared a few hours ahead of time and kept at room temperature.)

8. To serve, spoon dollops of whipped coconut cream atop the pineapple wedges and sprinkle with toasted coconut. Serve with the remaining whipped coconut cream and toasted coconut on the side.

DATE CAKE WITH CARAMEL ICING

3 tablespoons sliced almonds, for garnish

DATE MIXTURE

8 ounces (227g) pitted Medjool dates

1¼ cups water

1½ sticks (180g) unsalted butter, cut into pieces, softened, plus more for the pan

1 teaspoon baking soda (see Tip, below)

CAKE BATTER

2⅓ cups (345g) all-purpose flour, plus more for the pan

1 teaspoon baking soda

2 teaspoons ground cardamom

½ teaspoon fine sea salt

1 cup (200g) packed dark brown sugar

2 large eggs

1 teaspoon vanilla extract

ICING

6 tablespoons (60g) unsalted butter

6 tablespoons (52g) dark brown sugar

3 tablespoons whole milk

½ to ⅔ cup (65g to 95g) confectioners' sugar

TIP

Note that baking soda goes into the warm date mixture in addition to the cake batter. This step helps mellow the acidity of the dates.

I love the combination of dates with cardamom—the essential dessert spice of the subcontinent. Their warm flavors here make this cake a wonderful conclusion to an Indian meal. The dates imbue the cake with moisture and sweetness, while the caramel icing makes it incredibly irresistible! I recommend making this the morning before you serve it so the flavors have a chance to meld.

1.   Preheat the oven to 350°F. Butter and flour a 9-inch round cake pan.

2.   Place the almonds on a small baking sheet. Toast the almonds in the oven for 6 to 8 minutes. Immediately turn them out onto a plate to cool. Set aside.

3.   **Make the date mixture:** Place the dates and water in a 2-quart saucepan. Bring to a boil over high heat. Reduce the heat to low, cover, and simmer the dates until soft, about 5 minutes. Promptly transfer the mixture to a food processor and puree it until smooth.

4.   Pour the warm date puree into the bowl of a stand mixer with a paddle attachment. (Alternatively, you can pour it into a bowl and use a spoon to mix by hand.) Add the butter and the baking soda and mix slowly until the butter melts and blends into the date mixture, 3 to 5 minutes. Allow the mixture to cool to lukewarm.

5.   **Meanwhile, prepare the cake batter:** In a medium bowl, sift together the flour, baking soda, cardamom, and salt.

6.   When the date-butter mixture has cooled a bit, add the brown sugar and mix thoroughly. Add the eggs one at a time, mixing each until combined before adding the next, then add the vanilla. With the mixer on low (or using a spoon), gradually add the dry ingredients, mixing just until thoroughly incorporated.

recipe continues

7.   Pour the batter into the prepared pan. Bake in the center of the oven for 45 to 50 minutes, until dark golden and puffed and when you touch it, your finger leaves a light indentation (it should not be jiggly at all); a knife or toothpick inserted in the center should come out clean.

8.   Remove the cake from the oven and let it cool in the pan for 10 minutes, then turn it out onto a cooling rack and let it cool completely.

9.   **Make the icing:** When the cake has cooled, melt the butter in a heavy 2-quart saucepan over medium heat. Stir in the brown sugar and reduce the heat to low. Cook, stirring occasionally, just until the butter and sugar become thick, shiny, and a little stringy, about 2 minutes. Stir in the milk and increase the heat to medium. Cook, stirring constantly, just until the mixture comes to a boil. Remove from the heat and let it cool to lukewarm. Whisk in the confectioners' sugar, several tablespoons at a time, until the mixture is smooth, holds its shape, and has lightened some in color.

10. Let the glaze cool completely, then spread it over the top of the cake. Sprinkle with the toasted almonds and let it sit for at least 30 minutes before serving. This cake keeps well, covered at room temperature, for several days.

CARDAMOM COFFEE POTS DE CRÈME

This is one of my favorite desserts because it captures the rich flavor of South Indian "filter coffee," a uniquely delicious beverage similar to café au lait, except that the chicory adds a rich, malty note.

COFFEE

3 green cardamom pods, or ⅛ teaspoon ground cardamom

3 tablespoons coffee-chicory blend (see Tip)

¾ cup boiling water

CUSTARD

1½ cups heavy cream

½ cup (100g) sugar

6 large egg yolks

GARNISH (OPTIONAL)

½ cup heavy cream

½ teaspoon sugar

1 ounce semisweet chocolate, grated or shaved with a vegetable peeler

TIPS

• You can get a coffee-chicory blend from such brands as Cotha's Coffee or Café du Monde, both sold online. Or you can make it with your favorite medium to medium-dark roast beans; it just won't have the chicory notes.

• If your cardamom pods have been sitting in your cupboard for more years than you can remember, I suggest you get a fresh batch for this recipe! Or if your ground cardamom is fairly fresh, you can use that in a pinch.

1. Preheat the oven to 300°F.

2. **Prepare the coffee:** Gently crush the cardamom pods with the side of a knife. Remove the dark seeds and discard the pods. Place the seeds into a mortar and pestle or spice grinder and grind them finely.

3. Combine the cardamom and coffee in a coffee filter set inside a pour-over cone. Set the cone over a mug and carefully pour the boiling water into it. (A French press would also work.) Set the brew aside.

4. **Make the custard:** Pour the cream into a 3-quart saucepan over medium heat and warm it, stirring frequently, until bubbles form around the edge of the pan, 5 to 8 minutes. Add the brewed coffee and ¼ cup (50g) of the sugar and stir until the sugar dissolves. Remove from the heat.

5. In a medium bowl, whisk the egg yolks with the remaining ¼ cup (50g) sugar until well combined. Slowly add the cream mixture, whisking constantly so it doesn't curdle.

6. Divide the custard equally among six 4-ounce ramekins. Place a paper towel in an 11 × 14 baking dish and set the ramekins on it so they won't slide. Pour boiling water into the baking dish until it reaches halfway up the sides of the ramekins. Cover the baking pan tightly with foil and bake for 30 minutes, or until the custards are set. The edges will be firm but the centers should be slightly jiggly. Remove the baking dish from the oven and carefully transfer the ramekins to a cooling rack (I use rubber-tipped tongs).

7. When cool, refrigerate for 2 hours, or up to overnight before serving.

8. **Prepare the garnish, if desired:** Whip the cream and sugar using an electric mixer until moderately stiff peaks form; refrigerate.

9. Allow the pots to sit at room temperature for about 20 minutes before serving. Top each with whipped cream and grated or shaved chocolate and serve.

BASICS

Here are the building blocks you will use throughout this book.
They include spice blends, ghee, chutneys, and tandoori
marinade. While almost all of these items are commercially
available, I highly recommend making them from scratch
so you can control the quality and attain the most delicious
results.

Having jars of premade spice blends will help
tremendously when you prepare Indian food. My blends are
carefully balanced and work beautifully with these dishes.
Commercial versions will have different proportions of spices,
so I cannot promise you'll be as thrilled with the results if
you use them instead. The same is true for the chutneys and
tandoori marinade; you can purchase these items, but they
often contain additives and won't have the same nuanced
taste of homemade.

Everything in this chapter has a specific purpose,
carefully detailed in recipes throughout the book. Yet they
can each be used to enhance your daily diet—a sprinkle of
garam masala in a pot of beans, a dab of chutney on a piece of
fish, a marinade for grilling chicken. They can be handy tools
for putting a little Indian flavor on your plate.

NORTH INDIAN GARAM MASALA

2 tablespoons freshly ground black pepper

2 tablespoons ground cinnamon

2 tablespoons ground cloves

2 tablespoons ground cardamom

TIPS

• Garam masala is commercially available and is an acceptable substitute, but be aware that some contain significant amounts of cumin and coriander, which will give you a different flavor result and won't deliver the same warm-sweet taste of this recipe.

• This recipe calls for all pre-ground spices, but if you choose to grind your whole spices, just be sure the final volumes are equal.

Garam masala means "warm spices," and this mixture is named as such because it adds a warm spice note without any harsh red chili heat. This classic North Indian version is characterized by cinnamon, cardamom, clove, and black pepper. It can also include cumin, nutmeg, mace, and bay leaf, depending on each family's preference, but it never involves turmeric or cayenne. It's used extensively in North Indian cooking, often sprinkled over a meat curry like Classic Saag with Crispy Paneer (page 110) at the end of cooking as a final flourish, causing its aromas to "bloom" in the residual heat of the dish. It can also be used as part of the masala that flavors dals and vegetable dishes. I'm giving you a very simple formulation, using mostly pre-ground spices—a great shortcut, assuming your spices are relatively fresh. You will want to keep a jar of this beautiful spice blend on hand for many of the recipes in this book, including Tangy Tamarind Chutney (page 233), Creamy Black Lentil Dal (page 138), and Tea-Braised Punjabi Chickpeas (page 145).

In a small bowl, combine the pepper with the cinnamon, cloves, and cardamom. Mix thoroughly. Transfer to an airtight jar and store away from the light for up to a year.

Kerala Garam
Masala

North Indian
Garam Masala

Madras Curry
Powder

KERALA GARAM MASALA

4 teaspoons fennel seeds

8 whole star anise pods, or
    4 teaspoons ground star anise

4 teaspoons ground cinnamon

4 teaspoons ground cloves

4 teaspoons ground cardamom

2 teaspoons ground nutmeg

TIPS

• This blend is not available commercially, so you will definitely need to mix your own.

• Fennel is so much more fragrant when freshly ground, and its full flavor is important to this mix; resist using pre-ground for this one.

• Star anise is easier to find whole than pre-ground; that's why I recommend freshly grinding this spice.

This mixture is very different from its more famous cousin North Indian Garam Masala (page 222), so I don't recommend using them interchangeably. While both contain the cinnamon-clove-cardamom trio, Kerala Garam Masala also has significant amounts of star anise and fennel, which lend a sweet licorice-like fragrance to classic Kerala meat dishes such as Rich Kerala Egg Roast (page 161) and Peppery Beef Curry (page 166). Its flavor profile also makes it well-suited to sweets, so I put it in my Chocolate Tart with Cashew Crust (page 210), Chocolate Pistachio Shortbread (page 204), and Marmalade Saffron Squares (page 206). This mix is so heavenly and heady, you will love adding it to your spice collection. *See photograph on page 223.*

1. Place the fennel seeds in an electric spice grinder and grind to a fine powder. Tip it into a small bowl. Grind the star anise pods to a fine powder and add that to the bowl.

2. Add the remaining ingredients and combine thoroughly.

3. Transfer to an airtight jar and store away from the light for up to 1 year.

MADRAS CURRY POWDER

9 teaspoons coriander seeds

6 teaspoons black peppercorns

6 teaspoons fennel seeds

5 teaspoons cumin seeds

1 teaspoon cayenne

1 teaspoon ground turmeric

½ teaspoon ground cinnamon

½ teaspoon ground cloves

½ teaspoon ground cardamom

TIPS

• I use a combination of freshly ground whole spices and pre-ground, but you could use all whole spices if you prefer, as long as the quantities match.

• While I don't usually grind coriander seeds, they give this blend an extra boost of flavor.

Named for the city in Tamil Nadu that now goes by Chennai, this blend was originally popularized and exported by the British during the colonial era to send a taste of India back home to England. It wasn't embraced by Indian cooks during colonial times, because they seasoned each dish differently, based on recipes passed down for generations. Despite falling in and out of fashion in Britain, Madras curry powder has endured as the curry powder of choice in countries around the world, and it has a spot in every supermarket in America (though many of them contain loads of turmeric and fenugreek, giving them a sharp, bitter taste). But today, maybe out of nostalgia, Madras curry powder is being reclaimed and reinvented by Indians and non-Indians alike and is gaining a new level of respect as a distinct peppery South Indian spice blend that deserves a place in our pantries. I've had my own journey with it as a cook—first rejecting it, then reaching for it, appreciating it as a shortcut to flavoring soups and meat dishes. This is my formulation, which is potent but balanced with a nice peppery bite. *See photograph on page 223.*

1. Place the coriander, pepper, fennel, and cumin seeds in an electric spice grinder and grind to a very fine powder.

2. In a small bowl, combine the freshly ground spices with the cayenne, turmeric, cinnamon, cloves, and cardamom and blend thoroughly.

3. Transfer to an airtight jar and store away from the light for up to 1 year.

PANCH PHORON

2 tablespoons cumin seeds

2 tablespoons brown or black mustard seeds

2 tablespoons nigella seeds (kalonji)

1 tablespoon fennel seeds

1 tablespoon fenugreek seeds

The name of this spice blend from eastern India means "five spices" in Bengali. Unlike other Indian masalas, this one is made of whole seeds and always includes the same group: cumin, mustard, nigella, fennel, and fenugreek. Frequently these whole spices are sizzled in a tarka with oil or ghee and used to season dals, fish, or vegetables. This combination imparts an earthy, faintly bitter note to the food. Some cooks use equal proportions of all the spices, but my version has a little less fennel and fenugreek seeds because their flavors can be strong.

In a small bowl, combine all the spices and mix thoroughly. Transfer to an airtight jar and store away from the light for up to a year.

FAVORITE TANDOORI MARINADE

MASALA

3 medium garlic cloves, coarsely chopped

2 teaspoons chopped ginger

1 tablespoon ground coriander

1 teaspoon ground cumin

¾ teaspoon Kashmiri chili powder (see Tip)

¼ teaspoon sweet paprika

¼ teaspoon North Indian garam masala, store-bought or homemade (page 222)

3 tablespoons whole milk Greek-style yogurt

2 teaspoons tomato paste

1 teaspoon fresh lemon juice

1 tablespoon neutral oil

½ teaspoon fine sea salt

TIPS

• If you don't have Kashmiri chili powder, use a mixture of 3 parts sweet paprika to 1 part cayenne. Make extra and store it for future use.

• To make the marinade vegan, substitute cashew yogurt for Greek yogurt.

SERVING

• Use for making Tandoori Roasted Chicken with Charred Lemon and Onion (page 153) and Tandoori Cauliflower Steaks (page 105).

• It's ideal for marinating meats, vegetables, and paneer before grilling.

I've played around with tandoori marinades a lot over the years, and I landed on this super-quick, super-delicious version as my favorite. Yogurt is used in tandoori marinades because it gently tenderizes the meat before it is traditionally threaded on long skewers and lowered into a blasting hot tandoor (a large jar-shaped oven made of clay, with hot coals at the bottom). You don't need the oven, though, to enjoy the tangy, full flavor of this marinade.

Combine all the ingredients in a mini food processor or blender and blend to make a smooth paste. You'll need to scrape down the sides several times to make sure the ingredients blend well. Refrigerate if not using immediately. This will keep for up to a week in the refrigerator.

Tangy Tamarind
Chutney (page 233)

Vibrant Cilantro
Chutney

VIBRANT CILANTRO CHUTNEY

3 cups coarsely chopped cilantro leaves and tender stems

½ cup chopped white or yellow onion

1 large garlic clove, chopped

1 teaspoon chopped ginger

1 teaspoon minced serrano, jalapeño, or Thai bird chili

½ teaspoon ground cumin

¾ teaspoon fine sea salt, or to taste

½ teaspoon sugar

3 tablespoons plain whole milk Greek-style yogurt

4 teaspoons fresh lemon juice, or to taste

TIPS

• Cilantro can be gritty, so be sure to wash it well. If the first rinsing releases a lot of sand, rinse it a second time. Spin or gently pat the sprigs dry, and you're ready to go.

• To switch it up, add ¼ cup mint leaves or dill.

• This chutney keeps for up to 3 days in the refrigerator.

SERVING

• Pair with chaat snacks, such as Crispy Kale Pakoras (page 59) and Sweet Potato and Onion Bhaji (page 56).

• Serve with grilled chicken or fish, or with Lamb Scallion Kofta (page 53).

• Dollop it on your Potato Bonda Burger (page 120) or any sandwich.

Zesty and bright, this condiment is like a fresh salsa, bursting with flavor and meant to be eaten up quickly. It's one of the sauces you get with your street-food snacks in India, but it's so versatile you'll want to smear it on sandwiches and spoon it over fish.

Combine all of the ingredients in a food processor or blender and process until the mixture is thoroughly combined and resembles a pourable pesto. Add water, a tablespoon at a time, if needed to keep the mixture moving. Taste for seasoning, and adjust the lemon or salt according to your taste.

PICKLED RED ONION

1 medium red onion, peeled

¾ cup hot water

¼ cup apple cider vinegar

1 tablespoon sugar

¼ teaspoon cumin seeds

1 teaspoon fine sea salt

TIPS

• A mandoline or food processor with a thin slicing blade works well for cutting the onions, but a very sharp knife can also do the job.

• I prefer to slice the rings into half-moons, rather than thin radial segments, because the thickness is more consistent.

SERVING

• Scatter these over Warm Chickpea Salad with Cool Lime Cucumbers (page 92) or Cilantro-Mint Potato Salad (page 91), or put them on your Potato Bonda Burgers (page 120).

• Add them to avocado toast or a grain bowl.

Quick-pickled onions are a cinch to make and add the perfect bright jolt of acidity to sandwiches and salads. They pickle in the time it takes to make the rest of your meal, or you can prepare them ahead of time. I like to make mine a little Indian by adding cumin seeds, but you could amp up the flavor by also adding coriander seeds, black peppercorns, or dried red chili flakes.

1. Halve the onion lengthwise and trim off the top and root ends. With a very sharp knife or in a food processor, slice the onion crosswise into thin ⅛-inch half-moons (you should have about 2 cups).

2. In a medium bowl, combine the hot water and vinegar, add the sugar, cumin seeds, and salt, and stir to dissolve. Add the onion slices and submerge them in the vinegar mixture. Set aside at room temperature until ready to use, ideally 1 hour. These may be stored in a glass jar in the refrigerator for up to a week.

GHEE

4 sticks (1 pound) unsalted butter

TIPS

- Always use a clean, dry utensil when scooping it out, to avoid contamination and thus spoilage.

- It's easier to see when the milk solids begin to brown if you use a light-colored pan.

- Don't hurry the process or you risk burning the solids or not eliminating all the water, which could cause the ghee to spoil prematurely.

Ghee is simply butter that has been simmered until all the water has evaporated out of it and the milk solids have lightly browned—a process that makes it both shelf-stable and nutty tasting. It is similar to clarified butter, except clarified butter is strained of all particulates, hence "clarified." Brown butter is a closer analog, as both allow the milk particles to turn brown and contribute a caramel-y flavor. Store-bought ghee is a nice convenience, but I find it never has the same rich flavor of homemade. Whether you make it or buy it, a key benefit of cooking with ghee is it has a higher smoke point and won't burn the way butter does. It works well for making tarkas because they require the fat medium to be very hot for a sustained time while all the spices and aromatics sizzle. Once you start cooking with this golden ingredient, you'll discover not only how tasty it is in tarkas but also how it can take simple things like eggs, toast, popcorn, and risotto into another flavor zone! It doesn't require refrigeration, but it should be stored away from the light. I keep mine in a pint-size mason jar in the pantry so it's always soft, spreadable, and ready to go.

1. Set a clean 2-cup, heatproof glass jar into a metal bowl. The bowl will catch any drips when you tip the hot ghee into the jar.

2. Melt the butter in a 10-inch enamel or stainless steel sauté pan over medium to medium-low heat (just warm enough to keep it gently sputtering). Watch carefully and stir occasionally. After 10 to 12 minutes, the surface will change from large bubbles to a fine foam, at which point it is almost done. It will also make less noise since most of the water has boiled out. Check the color of the milk solids on the bottom of the pan by pushing the foam aside. When they turn golden brown, immediately remove the pan from the heat and pour the ghee into the jar, brown solids included (they add flavor). Cool, then cover; it will solidify and turn an opaque golden color. Store away from the light at room temperature for up to 6 months or in the refrigerator for up to 10 months.

TANGY TAMARIND CHUTNEY

2 teaspoons cumin seeds

CHUTNEY

¼ cup tamarind paste or concentrate

1 cup packed dark brown sugar

12 slices ginger (⅛ inch thick)

1 teaspoon fine sea salt

1¾ cups water

½ teaspoon North Indian garam masala, store-bought or homemade (page 222)

TIPS

• A trick for measuring tamarind is to smear a few drops of oil inside the measuring cup before pouring in the tamarind. This helps it slip out without sticking.

• Look for jarred tamarind paste or concentrate with a molasses-like texture. See Souring Agents on page 37.

SERVING

• This is a great dipping sauce for Crispy Kale Pakoras (page 59) and Sweet Potato and Onion Bhaji (page 56).

• Drizzle over Roasted Asparagus with Tamarind and Crispy Shallots (page 102) or grilled eggplant.

Tamarind chutney is one of the best uses of tamarind on the planet! A favorite condiment for Indian snacks and street food, this chutney showcases the fruit's date-like depth and tangy acidity, and balances them with brown sugar sweetness and the woody flavors of ginger and cumin. For all that complex flavor, it's actually very easy to make and it keeps a long time. It's a fantastic accompaniment to crispy fried food, but it's also terrific drizzled over roasted vegetables. *See photograph on page 228.*

1. In a small frying pan over medium heat, toast the cumin seeds, stirring and shaking the pan frequently, until they turn a darker shade of brown, release their fragrance, and smoke just a little, which will take 2 to 3 minutes. Stay close; you don't want them to burn. Tip the cumin seeds onto a plate so they immediately stop toasting. After a few minutes, when they are cool, grind them to a powder in a mortar and pestle or spice grinder.

2. **Make the chutney:** Combine the toasted cumin, tamarind paste, brown sugar, ginger, salt, and water in a 2-quart saucepan and bring to a boil over high heat. Reduce the heat to medium-low so the mixture is simmering at a lively rate and cook until it is a little thicker than soy sauce, about 20 minutes (it will thicken a lot more after it cools).

3. Remove the mixture from the heat and take out and discard the ginger slices. Stir in the garam masala and transfer the chutney to a heatproof glass jar with a tight-fitting lid. Cool and store in the refrigerator for up to 6 months.

Acknowledgments

This book has been percolating in me for years, but I credit Susan Herrmann Loomis, renowned cookbook author and collaborator extraordinaire, with getting it out of my head and onto the page. Susan is a brilliant culinary talent, walking encyclopedia of food, my trusted recipe consultant, a steady voice on the other end of the phone (in Paris!), and now my friend, and words cannot capture my appreciation of her. I am also grateful for my astute literary agent, Jane Dystel, for putting the two of us together and for convincing me to commit to this book. And my thanks to Miriam Goderich at the Dystel, Goderich & Bourret agency.

At Clarkson Potter, I'm beyond grateful to my editor, Jennifer Sit, for seeing the potential in my idea, for molding my manuscript into shape, and for always pushing me to go deeper. The design team, Stephanie Huntwork and Ian Dingman, were a pleasure to collaborate with; thank you for your inspiring vision! My deep gratitude to the first-rate editorial and production teams: editorial assistant Bianca Cruz, copy editor Kathy Brock, production editor Chris Tanigawa, and production manager Kim Tyner. And to everyone who worked so hard to get the word out, you're amazing: director of publicity Kate Tyler, marketer Monica Stanton and publicist Natalie Yera at Clarkson Potter; and Ilana Harkavy and the creative team at Nailed It Media.

My heartfelt thanks to the photography crew: the supremely talented photographer Eva Kolenko, who makes it all look effortless; her assistant Brad Knilans; the gifted food stylist Emily Caneer; her assistant Carrie Beyer; and brilliant prop stylist Ayesha Patel for her exquisite taste in props and thoughtful culinary input. And to the companies who generously provided cookware, thank you Le Creuset, All-Clad, and Made In.

From Maya Kaimal Foods, LLC, I'm grateful to Chip Baird, Alison Minter, Hemanshu Patel, Jane Pemberton, and Leslie Fuda at North Castle Partners for their crucial support of this project. A special shout-out to my dear friend and collaborator of fourteen years, chef Jessica Bard, who shares my wavelength and always has my back. And thanks to chef Devika Narula for contributing her great energy and culinary inspiration to the business and the book. My sincere thanks to Varant Minassian and Perry Abbenante for giving me the room to write this book, and Albert Valdes, for the sage advice. And to everyone at Maya Kaimal Foods, Jeff Newton, Louis Riccelli, Rod Fontenot, Matt Cacho, Andrew Bellisano, Steve Ihme, Rachel Russo-Mas, Sarah Dalzell, Joe Quattrucci, and Stephanie Massarelli (and the much-missed Elaine Delsol), I appreciate everything you do.

To these incredible humans whose personal and professional advice I cherish: Margo True, Patricia Fabricant, Kate Crow, Leslie McNeil, Susan Spungen, and Katie Calhoun—what a gift to be able to tap these brains. For recipe ideas and background research, my true thanks to Susan Westmoreland, Chelsea Ringquist, Nisha and Padma Krishnamoorthy, Syamala Surendranathan, Yoga Kalyanam, and Mira Menon. And thank goodness for my testers, whose feedback on the recipes was invaluable: Asya Ollis, Christian Crouch, Martha Gallagher, and Margo True.

I am eternally grateful to my parents, Lorraine and Chandran, for encouraging me to pursue my passion for food and art. I'm sorry my father didn't get to see this book completed, but I felt his presence at every step. My Aunty Kamala was also with me in spirit as I cooked these recipes. Thank you to my siblings and their spouses, Padma Kaimal, Narayan Kaimal, Andy Rotter, and Elissa Grad, who are my touchstones in food and life. Lastly and with a full heart, an enormous thank-you to my husband, Guy, for his unwavering belief in me, and to my beautiful daughters, Lucy and Anna, for giving me the love and support I needed, and then some.

Index

Published in the United States by Clarkson Potter/
Publishers, an imprint of Random House, a division
of Penguin Random House LLC, New York.
ClarksonPotter.com

CLARKSON POTTER is a trademark and POTTER
with colophon is a registered trademark of Penguin
Random House LLC.

Photographs on page 13 are courtesy of the author
except for bottom center, copyright © Zubin Shroff.

Library of Congress Cataloging-in-Publication Data
Names: Kaimal, Maya, author. | Kolenko, Eva,
photographer.
Title: Indian flavor every day : simple recipes
and smart techniques to inspire / Maya Kaimal ;
photography by Eva Kolenko.
Description: New York : Clarkson Potter, 2023 |
Includes index.
Identifiers: LCCN 2022021387 (print) | LCCN
2022021388 (ebook) | ISBN
9780593235065 (hardcover) | ISBN
9780593235072 (ebook)
Subjects: LCSH: Cooking, Indic—Kerala style.
Classification: LCC TX724.5.I4 K225 2023 (print) |
LCC TX724.5.I4 (ebook)
| DDC 641.5954—dc23/eng/20220715
LC record available at https://lccn.loc
.gov/2022021387
LC ebook record available at https://lccn.loc
.gov/2022021388

ISBN 978-0-593-23506-5
Ebook ISBN 978-0-593-23507-2

Food stylist: Emily Caneer
Prop stylist: Ayesha Patel
Photography assistant: Brad Knilans
Food stylist assistant: Carrie Beyer
Editor: Jennifer Sit
Editorial assistant: Bianca Cruz
Designer: Ian Dingman
Production editor: Christine Tanigawa
Production manager: Kim Tyner
Compositors: Merri Ann Morrell and Hannah Hunt
Copy editor: Kathy Brock
Marketer: Monica Stanton
Publicist: Natalie Yera

Printed in China

Cover photographs by Eva Kolenko

10 9 8 7 6 5 4 3 2

First Edition